ANT ACTS & BUILDS

SNAKE SLEEPS & RULES

The 9 Imperatives to Build A High-Performing Team

SRINIVASAN. T

STARDOM BOOKS

www.StardomBooks.com

STARDOM BOOKS, LLC
112, Bordeaux Ct,
Coppell, TX 75019

Copyright © 2023 by Srinivasan. T

This book is copyright under the Berne Convention.
No reproduction without permission.
All rights reserved.

The right of Srinivasan. T to be identified as the author of this work has been asserted by him in accordance with sections 77 and 78 of the Copyright, Designs and Patents Act, 1988.

FIRST EDITION JANUARY 2023

STARDOM BOOKS

A Division of Stardom Alliance
112, Bordeaux Ct,
Coppell, TX 75019

www.stardombooks.com

Stardom Books, United States
Stardom Books, India

The author and publishers have made all reasonable efforts to contact copyright-holders for permission, and apologize for any omissions or errors in the form of credits given. Corrections may be made to future editions.

ANT
ACTS & BUILDS

SNAKE
SLEEPS & RULES

Srinivasan. T

p. 205
cm. 13.5 X 21.5

Category:
BUS071000 : Business & Economics: Leadership
BUS046000 : Business & Economics : Motivational
ISBN: 978-1-957456-17-1

DEDICATION

This book is dedicated to all my leaders who coached me and also to my team members who were coached by me in action-oriented leadership, and eventually became star leaders.

FOREWORD

Srini is a leader who has his head in the clouds and feet firmly planted in the ground. He has grown immensely over the last 12 years that I have known him as an ideator, mentor, and leader.

Not for him would empty words do. Peppered with numerous examples, lived wisdom and common sense, this book is an essence of Srini's life as a leader.

People who are getting into leadership roles, becoming skip-level managers, and dealing with challenges of team conflicts and politics will benefit from his practical advice.

You will not get theory and jargon. You'll get analogies and stories. You'll get cases of real office situations. And you'll find that you can relate to them from your own past experiences.

I congratulate Srini for putting his accumulated experience into words for the benefit of others. I'm sure this will be of immense use to future leaders.

Sumeet Mehta
Co-founder and CEO
LEAD

CONTENTS

ACKNOWLEDGMENTS		i
WHY I WROTE THIS BOOK		iii
INTRODUCTION		1

PART 1: A LEADER'S WISDOM TOOTH

1	LEARN BEFORE YOU LEAN	9
2	CREDIBILITY IS AN OUTCOME OF CAPACITY	27
3	DIRECTING AND DOING	45

PART 2: LETTING THE ANTHILL GROW

4	ACTIONS SPEAK LOUDER THAN ANECDOTES	65
5	WHAT YOU SEE, GROWS	83
6	EXTRACT AND EXHIBIT	101

PART 3: THE MASTER MODEL BEHIND SUCCESS

7	REAL MOTIVATION STEMS FROM CLARITY	121
8	IDEATION TO EXECUTION	139
9	C FOR CAPACITY, NOT COMPETITION	157
	CONCLUSION	175
	REFERENCES	187

ACKNOWLEDGMENTS

Growth holds a magnificent meaning. It nourishes aspiration in every individual. However, people often fail to act suitably while trying to satisfy their aspirations. There prevails a gap between aspiration for growth and action toward growth. This book is for aspiring leaders to understand the basics and importance of putting actions in sync with their aspirations. My journey as an author will be incomplete without a note of gratitude to the people who helped me and guided me in transforming my aspirations into actions and helped me grow from bottom to top.

My note of gratitude starts with my dad, Mr. Thimmarayan, who is a hard-core action-driven person even at the age of 75, and raised us amid all the difficulties of life.

I thank my brother, Mr. Sundaramoorthy, who diverted me from becoming a uniform service person to a people manager, and my better half, Mrs. Mahalakshmi, who stood by me in all my crazy decisions. She has been my spine, managing everything at home so that I can do everything I aspired to do.

I leave a special note to my team members who worked with me and took all the pain in learning the importance of action, have grown leaps and bounds in their careers, and got disciplined in their personal life too. Having spent more than five years in LEAD, I would not have written this book if I had not got an opportunity from LEAD's founders, Mr. Sumeet and Ms. Smita.

It has been indeed a pleasure to be an integral part of India's B2B EdTech Unicorn, which has been powering 3000+ K-12 Schools across India, delivering excellent education. I am thoroughly indebted to the whole team of LEAD for allowing me to implement all my learnings about the importance of action in building a high-performing team.

My customers are the real stars on my shoulders, and I take this opportunity to thank five key customers, Mr. Suribabu, Mr. Mahesh, Dr. Joseph Thomas, Mr. Basco Iraiyanbu, and Mr. Raja, for trusting the concept of an action-driven organization while growing their institutions.

Lastly, my Stardom partners were like my anchors. I thank Ranjitha and Atrayee, who believed in my words and pushed me to make a debut in this writing and publishing world.

This book holds many close-to-life narratives to give you a realistic approach toward leadership skills. Perfection is an illusion. It is true that no leader can be depicted as a perfect leader; however, this book will hone your leadership abilities to tackle this continuously changing market 'perfectly'.

WHY I WROTE THIS BOOK

Inspiration never comes in handy. You have to experience life while scripting some glorious success stories and also falling flat to reach a trivial target. Life bestows you with lessons, sometimes in the form of critical circumstances and sometimes through the variety of people you encounter on your journey to the top. And everything put together inspires you to leave a footprint on this mortal world. I am often tagged as a people manager and have helped build successful start-ups from scratch. 18+ years in the world of building businesses was not an easy job for me but, of course, enlightening. Whether conceiving an innovative idea about a product, chalking out an execution strategy, or cracking a deal with an irreplaceable client, I had the opportunity to work with and groom many budding leaders.

However, in the last five years, opportunities and challenges competed with each other. Even during the greatest achievements and the most challenging times, a few of my team members stood by me. They implemented my leadership strategies and became real role models for action-oriented leadership. My narrative of ant philosophy will remain incomplete without mentioning them and their growth stories. As everyone would endorse my views, leadership strategies to build high-performing teams are a crowded domain when it comes to writing and publishing a book on the topic. It is often considered a domain to be touched by the biggies in the market who had been inheriting that crown of leadership.

By sheer luck or coincidence, whatever you may call it, in my course of affairs, I was never gifted anything. Being from a humble background, I had to make my mark because leadership was something given to me as another task. Therefore, I could never conceive or idolize the idea of becoming that snake at the top of the anthill who would sleep and rule.

Writing a book was not my forte or first desire in life, but as I progressed in building some of the new-gen leaders, I was encouraged to pen down my philosophy. In my journey to become and remain the ANT, I was fortunate enough to inculcate this mindset into a handful of few who, in turn, inspired me to universalize my idea of leadership. And without thanking or mentioning the progress report of some of my team members, my writing journey would be incomplete.

So, let me begin with Naveen Rasineni. It was an arduous task to transform an abandoned B2B Edtech market into a strong customer base by building a highly productive team. However, Naveen understood and implemented my ideas about the importance of a customer-oriented service strategy. As a mentor, it gave me immense pleasure to see Swapnil Zarekar, a rockstar sales executive to have grown into a team leader and manage 60 rockstar sales members.

Somehow, if we see closely, we will understand that we all are given ample opportunities to grow in life. It actually depends on our own perspectives to grow. Suma. N is one of the best examples to prove that. She took up all the challenging roles as a learning spree and became a Project Manager in a fast-growing, high-expecting organization from being an inside sales executive.

Similarly, Saravanan. P could grow to manage 300-member multifunctional team by changing his complete working style at every level, learning and implementing the techniques fast. Believe me, he started by managing just five sales executives. Also, Abhijeet Tendulkar grew up to manage 150 multifunctional team members by taking similar learning. A little pride I could share as I think of Venu Gopal Reddy, who, from being an implementation expert, became a Lead Trainer for multiple customer-facing roles.

Ritika Chawla, from being someone who failed to connect and build trust with her first KDM, is now leading 100 people and is connecting with approximately 900 KDMs and continues building trust. As their mentor, I am further encouraged by seeing Prasanth Subramani, who grew to identify new markets, build high-value customers and build a team from scratch, while Himanshu Sharma, and Abhishek Sarbariya, are now exhibiting strong leadership skills in tough markets and nurturing new leaders under them.

I am not using appeasing tactics when I say that my people have encouraged me to write this book. In fact, the beginning chapter, Learn Before You Lean, is loaned from my experience with Ashok Pemmi. Similarly, my ideas about Actions Speak Louder Than Anecdotes are borrowed from living examples like Saleem Mohammed, Kailash Gupta, and Ananya Shandilya, who could leave their past glory and took the brave decision to join hands in building a new business vertical. Every chapter of this book has been scripted with a role model in mind. Thrusting leadership skills and talents in an established business house carries one kind of story; however, the narrative takes a dramatic shift when it comes to budding businesses. I am glad to see that this Ant Philosophy is able to thrive even in the newest members like Sukesh Thogaru and Ashwini Chikmath.

As I begin to carve a new niche in the world of writing and publishing, I would quote Ernest Hemingway—*We are all apprentices in a craft where no one ever becomes a master.* Even in my pursuit of leadership, I always wish to remain an apprentice so that my learning process never stops for a moment. The team I have built in the past, and the people I have been working with, have always imparted me with the right push to grow in my personal and professional life.

I believe in my leadership strategies and have found their worth by witnessing many people making a smooth transition in their growth curve. Leadership skills or strategies can never be generalized in a world that is volatile, uncertain, and ambiguous. As I found my perspectives making me comfortable with ambiguity, it was indeed an excellent idea to universalize them through this book.

Writing is an art, and no one needs a specific or bookish reason to write a book; however, when you see your ideas bringing in a better change, it is worth publishing your idea. There are umpteen books in the market to preach about leadership skills. Management jargons, well-segmented topics, series of flowcharts, and hefty case studies; most of the books give a thorough feeling of a real-time workshop training for honing your leadership skills. They are indeed beneficial as you get lectured without even stepping out of your cozy couch.

However, as I nourished my reading habits, I found storytelling or creative nonfiction always imparts a better learning experience.

So, instead of delving into the same workshop/teaching style of writing a book on leadership, I chose a narrative of my own. Free-flowing, and a little far from the academic touch, my writing style intends to grab the pain points first and then provide a suitable solution. With many hypothetical case scenarios, I am sure the readers will be able to relate to the problems that prevail in an organizational setting. So, dive into my Ant-Snake strategy of building leadership skills and unleash the leadership potential that is latent within you.

INTRODUCTION

Have you ever lent a thought over ants? The present time paces like a greased lightning while we ricochet between different episodes of success and failure, and until a situation arises that gives us ants in our pants (metaphorically), we hardly think about that trivial form of life on this planet. However, considering their survival strategy, we humans have a lot to learn.

In 2016, Jim Rohn, the famous American motivational speaker, proposed *The Ant Philosophy* in his bestselling audiobook, 'The Day That Turns Your Life Around'. Interestingly, ants' survival strategy can impart the essence of leading a successful career, both as an individual contributor in an organization and also as a leader.

Ants never quit! At some point in time, we all would have playfully tried to block the chain of moving ants; however, the ants would have looked for some other way. They will move left, right, or go under your finger gaps, but they will never stop the progression. Nothing can deter them from their goal. Come what may, they will find another way to reach their destination.

Quite the opposite of this ant's philosophy, in the present times, we are often confused about setting our ultimate goals. Some of us wish to harvest only the inherent skills and earn accolades in niche domains, while many wish to upskill and diversify through constant learning. The millennial is trapped in the gig economy's ideology and moonlighting to earn better. On the same note, with ample opportunities thriving around the corner, quitting one job for another has become a regular affair. And in this pursuit of shifting from one organization to another, although we do keep a watch on the paycheck, we tend to overlook one of the significant hurdles in our growth curve. We are NOT climbing the ladder of growth; instead, we remain stagnant at the same stage while the ladder keeps changing. That's all. Essentially, instead of upskilling ourselves to the next level of the hierarchy and embracing general leadership skills, we tend to remain insulated in our comfort zone.

Sometimes, it seems fruitful to stick to one's inherent skills, be it technical or administrative; however, the final outcome is often sour in the long run. We don't realize that the marrow of growth and development rots in silence in this undying desire to feel comfortable. Moreover, until we climb the ladder, we can never reach the top of the hierarchy and grab the glorious hat of leadership skills.

Right now, we are thriving within a dog-eat-dog kind of competition where each day pushes us to an entirely unknown domain of challenges. Unhindered innovation, continuous evolution of technology, and volatile market have become some of the critical challenges for every organization, both at an individual level and for the top leaders. We need effective management and decision-making skills at every level to survive in this competitive world.

The more we grow in our career graph, the better we fathom the different features of the same challenges and, in turn, become capable of strategizing a newer way to combat them. However, combating challenges at an individual level and as a leader are two different avenues to tread.

If we wish to see ourselves at the top of the hierarchy, we must inculcate some crucial leadership traits to lead a team and reap benefits for the whole organization. Like ants, a leader cannot quit progressing toward the organizational goal. Crafting a fool-proof vision, setting realistic goals, empowering the human resource to achieve that goal, and strategizing overall profit for the organization remain the ultimate motto in a leader's life.

In the present times, curiosity, creativity, credibility, and being comfortable with ambiguity are must-have leadership skills. Leaders have to become the catalyst for change when the world is changing so drastically. And that change has to be incorporated within personal perspective as well as organizational performance. Relying on educational achievements and past accolades can never build leaders for the future. Past is always beyond reach, while the future is always prone to change; it is only the present time where the leaders have to build their credibility through their actions. Leaders of this millennial era must remain the anchor who can bring people of varied skills together and construct a collective effort to build a product, keeping the customers in mind. People, product, and process; channelizing everything in cohesion with each other is one of the most challenging tasks for present-day leaders.

When the future is uncertain, and the world needs the leader to be a change champion, then the leader must be capable of thinking ahead of time. Much like ants thinking of summer during winter and planning for winter during the summer, leaders have to strategize their moves well in advance by grasping the stark realities of the market.

Now, leaders are often haunted by murky doubts like — Does the organization have the right set of people to perform the assigned task? Is the product competitive enough? Are the customers happy? On the same note, leaders face the harshest challenge in the form of organizational politics. Keeping an organization actively performing needs constant participation from its leaders. So, how much participation is enough? The answer is, *All-you-possibly-can!*

Effective leaders are like ants; they always act and build. If you observe an anthill closely, there is a continuous commotion. Ants are always busy doing something. A chain will enter it while another chain of ants will come out, reflecting upon the continuity of performance. An organization's functioning is quite synonymous with an anthill. It is more convoluted and complex as we dig deeper. Every individual holds a distinct and defined role to accomplish.

Moreover, as every individual strives toward the same goals, the organization grows stronger. Coming to think of the anthill; interestingly, the fate of the anthill drastically changes as soon as a snake enters. Beyond the scope of mythological anecdotes of snakes living on an anthill, the ants-snakes-anthill concept produces a deeper understanding of leadership skills in an organizational setting. As soon as a snake enters the anthill, it stops growing, and the ants stop performing and eventually leave the mound for better prospects. But it is not like the snake demolishes an anthill. It will never do so because it uses the anthill for thermoregulation; nevertheless, the anthill stops growing in height as soon as the snake steps in.

While ants keep acting, the anthill keeps growing, much like how an organization keeps growing with continued performance, and as soon as a snake enters the scene, it hinders the growth. Snake just sits and relishes the comfort without giving two hoots to the growth of the anthill. If one takes a closer look, this simple anthill concept highlights leadership's pathological aspect: sleeping and ruling by creating fear and dominance. The situation of the snake being at the top is like maintenance rather than being growth-oriented.

No organization is built for maintenance; rather, it is the idea of growth that builds a business empire. Thus, having a snake at the top is fruitless, which invites nothing more than stagnancy. Any organization is built while amalgamating organizational culture with a high-performing team, innovative products, and a customer base. And it grows and fetches success in the market when the leader comprehends not only the changing nerves of the market but also the potential and loopholes in the team and the products. Sitting at the top like a snake on the top of an anthill might give the leader the temporary joy of holding the reign; however, it can neither account for a credible leader nor build a successful organization.

Building and retaining a highly efficient team amidst this atmosphere of creaking competition is a considerable challenge. On deeper analysis, the core leadership challenges remain the same whether a leader is building a nation, an MNC, or a startup.

Attracting, enabling, empowering, and retaining the best and the brightest talent to achieve the organizational goal are the prime objectives of an effective leader. If the organization is lucky enough to catch the right talent, the leader must ensure an open, fair, innovative, competitive, and meritocratic culture for the talent to grow further. In this tech-savvy environment, present-day leaders must teach and also gather a deep understanding of the evolving technology. Thus, continuous learning becomes an essential ingredient in a leader's to-do list. Even the best of talents would like to see their leaders well-equipped with knowledge and skills and hold the potential to solve problems.

Additionally, building credibility by exhibiting an action-oriented approach and encouraging participation from the whole team in decision-making adorns the leadership hat. A perfect leader has an appetite for innovation and a relentless desire to meet customer demands while keeping the entire team adaptable to change.

The prevailing challenges in the market have crafted a few essential tenets for making an effective leader.

- **Tenet 1**: Encourage constant learning among the leaders and team members.
- **Tenet 2**: A thorough understanding of the business, the goals, the kind of team needed to achieve the goal, the market niche, the customer base, product design, and the capacity to improvise.
- **Tenet 3**: Motivation through action. Leaders who wish to sleep and rule are no longer needed in any organization that wishes to grow.
- **Tenet 4**: Be action-oriented; conceive the idea of success and execute it till the end with active participation.
- **Tenet 5**: Focus on capacity building over competition.

These tenets demand the present-day leaders to move toward diversification while upholding uniqueness to succeed in this hungry-for-success business world. Constant upskilling and renovating the inherent capacity of the organization, team, and product rather than reinventing to win over a competitor have drawn much attention in the present times.

The business world is volatile, unsettled, competitive, and ambiguous. As change remains a constant companion, building a successful organization is never possible without acting toward the stipulated goal. Power, position, authority, and delegation are a fragment of leadership roles. The bigger and brighter picture demands credible leaders whose actions speak louder than words and who know what to delegate, when to delegate; whom to delegate and who also knows when to come out of that delegation role and work on the field. It is a product and customer-driven world, and the leaders must be agile to change.

As you delve into the following pages, each chapter shall drill deeper to unveil the essential qualities needed in present-day leaders. From building credibility as a leader to enhancing the capacity of the whole organization, the magic mantra of becoming an effective leader lies dormant inside every aspiring leader. You just have to shake it up a little.

> *"The challenge of leadership is to be strong, but not rude; be kind, but not weak; be bold, but not bully; be thoughtful, but not lazy; be humble, but not timid; be proud, but not arrogant; have humor, but without folly."*
> — Jim Rohn

PART 1

A LEADER'S WISDOM TOOTH

1

LEARN BEFORE YOU LEAN

Once upon a time, there lived a tribe in a village. The oldest man invariably became the wisest amongst all and eventually became the leader. A strict disciplinarian, the wise old man did not like or entertain any bending-the-rule phenomenon. Neither did he let any meddling with the existing system, nor did he wish to learn anything new or proceed to advancement. As years passed by, the nearby villages embraced the unique hues of change and eventually became more progressive with time.

However, the old man and his tribe were stuck within that same fragile and waning mindset. The old man kept leaning over his comfortable and yet limited knowledge while the world moved at lightning speed. Considering the shunted growth, many tribe members decided to move elsewhere, leaving behind the old man all alone, caged inside his preconceived notion. Once revered as a know-it-all personality, the old man suddenly became a half-witted burden for the whole tribe. His ignorance, bullheadedness, and unaccommodating attitude became a curse to growth and development. In a matter of time, the tribe members dethroned their leader only to move with the new tide of change.

As I narrate this slice of fiction, do you find an uncanny resemblance with our persisting organizational requirements? Every business, whether a startup or traditional setup, is flourishing amidst a constantly changing world. As the world changes, the knowledge domain widens, and thus, a plethora of information comes in. Now, is there a limit set to acquiring such information or knowledge?

Suppose I am a salesman, doing exceptionally great in cracking some big deals for my company. Do I need to learn anything about my organization's financial management or operational cost and management? The common misconception is to be a master of one rather than becoming a jack of all trades. In some contexts, it may fit well; however, if I am given the duty of leading a team of varied talents, I cannot shy away from knowing the basic details of every skill required to run my team or a company.

The world is witnessing an era of reskilling where the whole ideology of leadership is altered and redefined to thrive well in this constantly changing and competitive world. Continuous learning at the workplace has become the new norm, irrespective of your position. Whether you are an individual, an entry-level employee, or you are chairing the whole organization, you have to embrace the phenomenon of constant learning. It is often believed to be harder to learn new things when one grows old or climbs the ladder. Probably, it is because the pain of making mistakes or the fear of embarrassment doesn't wash away as quickly as it might have when we were younger. In the present scenario, where the market is swiftly changing its demand and supply continuum, leaders are bound to foster an environment of psychological safety where the team is supported and challenged enough to boost productivity.

How to do that? Many organizational behavioral scientists would ask the leaders to dial up their levels of empathy and humility to extract the best from the team rather than commanding it. However, what happens when leaders decide to remain in their cocoon of delegation without even understanding the problems cropping up in the changing market? What if the leaders do not know enough about the complexity of a situation or the team's potential?

Let's take the example of Blockbuster going out of business as they misjudged the rise of online streaming services, especially Netflix. Blockbuster was a video service organization that started by renting out VHS tapes. The company's core service moved from VHS to CDs, DVDs, Video Game rentals, and Blu-Ray discs as time progressed. Coincidentally, online streaming services like Netflix were slowly picking up the pace in major cities across the USA. Blockbuster had 9094 outlets across the mainland USA at the height of its popularity.

The management of Blockbuster miscalculated the speed at which the internet was encroaching and eventually delayed their foray into digital streaming services despite having the opportunity to buy out Netflix during its fledgling days. Soon enough, Netflix bought streaming rights to most successful sitcoms, dramas, and straight-to-DVD movies. This ensured an increased customer base for Netflix services which consequently witnessed the downfall of Blockbuster. Within five years, the once a big brand in the entertainment sector saw its 9000+ outlets reduced to two. Additionally, the company had accrued more than 900 million USD in debt, filing for bankruptcy.

No matter how big or small an organization is, even the highest-performing teams fail to strategize accurately without continuous learning. Blockbuster is an example of blatant overconfidence where the leaders failed to fathom the growing change. Decisions were made through a myopic lens without widening the information base. If delegation and authority are the weapons of a leader, confidence is one of the most precious gems a leader can have.

On the same note, the gem called confidence must be chiseled by acquiring more and more knowledge. Leaders who keep themselves abreast of recent advancements always make an informed decision and delegation. An organization is built on different pillars. A leader must know all the nuances of the business, be it sales or finance, production, and the volatile market and customer inclinations.

"Leadership and learning are indispensable to each other."
– John F. Kennedy.

Learning is a continuous process. In the growth curve of your career, when you are given the privilege of climbing the next step in the ladder of organizational hierarchy, it is a chance to see the business world from a different perspective. You would have started your career in the sales or PR department; however, when you are promoted to the administrative wing, you are given a chance to learn the brass tacks of production units, the financial prospects of the organization, and its operational cost.

Consider a standard organizational setting. At the entry-level, you had learned the sales tricks to crack a deal, and as your excellent people management skill gets noticed, you are promoted to lead the production unit. You are naive to this new department, but gradually widen your knowledge and get acquainted with the different lines of products your company manufactures.

Thus, at this second stage of your career, you are accomplished with sales skills and also understand product management. Your performance excels, you climb to the next level, and over time, you garner enough knowledge about all the supporting functions of an organization. In essence, with every step you take toward career growth, you are gifted with an opportunity to strengthen a new domain. Also, you turn capable enough to look back and find the flaws in the system. For example, if you are moved to the production department from the sales, you will now be capable of designing a better sales tactic while understanding the crucial details of the product.

Somehow, we all harbor a negative connotation with the phrase jack of all trades. It is more like becoming a wheeler-dealer who would sell anything to anyone by knowing little about everything around them and using tricks to get their way. However, the whole phrase is "A jack of all trades is a master of none, but often better than a master of one." Does it still ring a bell of pessimism?

A business is run through a complex set of wheels, where every wheel needs to be maintained using different tools. A leader needs an ongoing expansion of knowledge and skill sets while reinforcing what has been previously learned. A leader with a proven track record in sales and marketing cannot shy away from dealing with the financial dilemma that the company faces. While climbing the career ladder, if a potential leader learns the multifaceted aspect of running a business, he will have a thorough knowledge of operational management, the market scenario, and the customer base.

A true believer in continuous learning would accept its broad definition. Education can be formal or informal and structured or unstructured. A potential leader who desires to script a new definition of growth for his company can entertain traditional courses or observe more-experienced employees, asking for assistance with an unfamiliar topic. Exploring new and alternative work methods, studying, casual conversation, and practicing the use of a skill widen a leader's knowledge domain, thus making him the right fuel for the company's growth engine.

Precisely, an individual gets ample opportunity to learn, while the process of learning begins from self-learning. Any ingredient of growth is rooted initially within us. Let me share my way of learning anything new. Business meetings are significant sources of opportunities to grow. Whether you are attending the first meeting of your life or have become an accustomed player, every interaction opens a new door to learning something undone before. I always nurtured a habit of recording my meetings (with due permission, of course), irrespective of the nature and status of my client. I used to play my meeting recordings in my free time or while traveling for another project. My intention was only to analyze my answers along with the context of the meeting. The more I listened to them, and I could find out an alternative response that could have yielded a better outcome. Moreover, as I listened to the recording, I could comprehend the questions any future clients would ask me. As I kept revisiting my previous meetings' recordings, I could prepare myself better for my next meetings while learning to give better analogies.

If one observes the organizational hierarchy, the top leaders are very lone souls. However, if they wish to keep themselves grounded with the realities of the market, they must start learning from the team that goes to the ground level and grasps the accurate picture.

Learning from team members is the second aspect of learning. For example, if a single salesman of your company comes back to the office and reports about a new kind of product available in the market, the leader must not ignore his findings. You will never know how soon the new kind of product will become a formidable competitor for your company. Just because the news has come under the consideration of one team member, it doesn't mean it can be ignored. Every ounce of the challenge faced by the team members must be acknowledged, and the leader must try to collaborate while finding a solution.

Growth mindset pioneer and author of the book *Mindset*, Carol Dweck quoted, *"Individuals who believe their talents can be developed (through hard work, good strategies, and input from others) have a growth mindset. They tend to achieve more than those with a more fixed mindset (those who believe their talents are innate gifts)."* We all share a common goal in life – to excel in our professional front. And as soon as we enter the talent pool, we sense the throat-choking competition. Moreover, as we witness someone performing better than us, we tend to categorize successful people under the tag of favoritism.

On the contrary, anyone interested in self-growth would constantly seek the positive aspects of their successful peers. The question is not why someone else could do it better than you. The real trick is understanding someone else's strategies to reap success.

Let's take the simple example of a boardroom presentation. We all have that colleague who has an excellent command over language and knows how to make things look glittery. Similarly, there is always a handful of few in a team who are excellent in practical aspects of work but fail to present it well. Good communication skill is not everyone's forte; however, turning your flaws into an asset is always possible if you are ready to cope and learn new things with an open mind.

Instead of griping over a colleague's success, you should focus on finding his strength and incorporating it into your working style. Most of the time, ego comes into play when one wishes to learn from a peer. On the other hand, not every successful colleague will be interested in sharing their expertise with others. And then comes the role of observation. There is no better teacher than mere observation. Once you inculcate the habit of observation, you learn from every stratum and every fabric of life. As they say, there is no better teacher than life itself.

The fourth source of learning happens with close observation of our supervisors. We, as humans, are gluttons for appreciation. We tend to develop close associations with people who admire us and hardly disagree with our point of view. Our general outlook toward a strict supervisor is often negative because we fail to see the real benefits behind his course of actions or chosen words. A man or woman sitting at the top was not placed there just for fun or as a matter of inheritance. Even in a family-run business like Godrej's or Ambani's, the top management has to undergo rigorous training to fit into the shoes. If you want to climb to the pinnacle, you cannot escape from observing your supervisors. How do they work? How do they manage their time and handle the challenges in life? A good leader who is always approachable in turn becomes a good teacher. The leader's success and also failures can always be critical learning lessons.

There is a beautiful verse from Whitman's poem Debris that resonates well with our learning process.
"Have you learned the lessons only from those who admired you, were tender with you, and stood aside for you? Have you not learned great lessons from those who braced themselves against you and disputed passage with you?"

As business leaders, learning is essential for growth and development as there are always new skills to master and new technology to learn. A learned leader eventually empowers employees and creates a culture of professional development.

On the same note, continuous learning nurtures conviction within. Leadership is not about convincing a team to reach the organizational goal but about making the process smooth and worthwhile through conviction.

Let me dissect two hypothetical case scenarios while canvassing two kinds of leaders.

Mr. Parashuram has been newly appointed as the CEO of a publishing house. He has been an experienced player in the real estate business and had many accolades under his hat. However, the publishing house was a new domain where he needed to learn the basics and operational style. He was inducted, considering his success stories, but no one thought of looking into his credibility to run a publishing house. On the other hand, Mr. Parashuram took his position for granted and considered delegating the work to the lower management, who was well acquainted with the process. Initially, it worked well as the team understood delegation as the only task of a leader. But as soon as problems cropped up or a new change came into the market, Mr. Parashuram fell short of words and could not strategize a way out.

Moreover, his immediate subordinates failed to find suitable guidance. The leader's credibility came under the scanner in no time, and the team could sense the disharmony. Gradually, everyone became their own boss and started taking a call based on their aptitude. The air in the office turned hostile, and within a matter of a week Mr. Parashuram was declared unfit for his role.

Sooner or later, the publishing house had to find a better replacement. And this time, instead of hiring a high-profile candidate from the market, the management preferred to give a chance to an ingrown talent, Michelle. She had spent fifteen years with the company and had been in almost every department, even if for a short time. Over the years, she has gained experience in sales, marketing, and the editorial department. However, running an organization also needed her to know the other components. Instead of sitting in the newly provided cabin, she chose an alternative option.

She worked in cohesion with the production and finance head and thoroughly understood the prevailing problems and how to combat them. She participated in the whole team management process and encouraged every team member to shed light on the ongoing issues. Over a couple of months, the whole team accepted and enjoyed her participative leadership style, and productivity increased. Amidst all that, Michelle became a leader with a widened domain of knowledge who never delegated anything without having a thorough grasp of the problem.

Knowledge and experience bedeck our confidence further. In many cases, confidence has been found to have got mutated into arrogance among leaders. They remain so engrossed in their success stories that they fail to see the other way of handling situations or teams. Or, they just thought to put a full stop to their learning process. Any organization works on the premise of symbiotic relationships where there is a continuous flow of information between the teams and the leader. A learned leader is an asset, but an unapproachable intellectual leader is a massive barrier to a company's growth.

Mr. Parashuram remained a know-it-all kind of leader who did not see the necessity to learn tricks from his subordinates or anyone for that matter. At the same time, Michelle's approachable nature provided a positive impact on the whole team. Although she was uprooted from her core sales department, she became a true leader by understanding the team dynamics and probable sources of organizational politics and incorporating varied ways to run the organization.

As per Pareto's Principle, just 20 percent of our efforts lead to 80 percent of our desired results. Investing in learning and professional development pays off in dividends not only for you as a leader but also for the team and the company. A growth-oriented leader would appreciate the DISSS method of learning, i.e., Deconstruction-Selection-Sequencing-Stakes. In the learning process, the potential candidate must break the learning into smaller tasks and select which task to focus on.

In the above scenario, Michelle knew her deficiencies and focused on addressing that first. Later, one must determine the order in which to learn tasks for optimal performance. In Michelle's case, productivity was erratic due to the absence of a credible leader. So, she focused on proving her credibility to delegate by widening her knowledge base. Lastly, the stakes should be considered before committing to succeed. Mr. Parashuram's failure to run the company came as an opportunity to learn about the importance of learning in building strong leaders.

Present India is scripting a new tale of entrepreneurship that needs future leaders to embrace societal shifts. There are no static maps for availing success, nor can the leaders manage complexity by fixating on the details. The business world often draws an analogy with the short story, *On Exactitude in Science*. The cartographers appointed by the empire drew a detailed map, mile by mile, that covered the whole territory and led to the empire's downfall. Absurdity and unintended consequences build the story's frame, which present-day leaders must appreciate.

The 21st century is about reinvention and relevance, where our focus is on adjusting our way of thinking, learning, and doing. Leaders must be comfortable getting into the skin of perpetual beta mode by being receptive and able to learn. Considering the fast-paced world, the half-life of every skill is about five years. Thus, the leaders are responsible for renewing their perspective to secure the relevance of their organizations. The business world is bearing a networked creative economy where leaders who promote learning and who master fast, relevant, and autonomous learning are considered of superior worth. Wicked problems surround us, and leadership should be about enabling learning, both for the leaders and the team.

The need of the hour is to transfer from scalable efficiency to scalable learning because even with so much advancement and incorporation of technology, most companies remain underprepared for challenges. We must find ways to connect and participate in knowledge flows that challenge our thinking and allow us to discover new ways of connecting, collaborating, and getting work done faster, smarter and better. Customers are the most fruitful connection for any business. Learning your customers from the inside out is the most proficient way to crack a deal.

Till now, I have emphasized enough the importance of learning for our self-growth as a leader. Now, as a leader, you are bound to face two major problems; one with the team failing to crack a deal, and the other is about aligning the team with the organization's goal. Let's analyze the first problem in detail.

As a person from a sales background, I have often faced one critical situation: finding compelling reasons for a customer to sign with my product. The market is huge, and there is an umpteen number of players; then why and how should a customer choose you from that overabundance of options? If the sales team fails to find a compelling reason to convince a customer, there can never be a fruitful deal.

From my experience, I can say with utmost conviction that when customers express that they will get back to you, they are buying time to check out other options. Once the salesman learns the compelling reason for a customer to come in, he can tailor-make his products as per the prevailing demands. As a leader, one must teach the team to identify the reason for customer retention, to make the product meet the customer demands, and then build trust with the customers. Believe me; trust fosters amidst knowledge. A product or a company can crack any number of deals with the customer market once it proves its credibility even amidst the competition.

My foray into the Edtech industry was like building everything from scratch. I took every product and went to do personal pitching. With every interaction, I could locate the loopholes and kept refining the product. Trials and tribulations continued, but gradually I could make a standardized procedure about how to convince potential customers. Soon enough, my whole team was taught the nitty-gritty of making a compelling proposal. As the team grew, more and more ideas flew in, and innovation became our constant companion.

Over the years, I had to shift my focus from smaller clients to high-profile clients. With constant learning, I could widen the knowledge base of my whole team, so much so that, in a few years' time, my team could handle the groundwork while I concentrated on making bigger deals. High-profile clients provided me with newer and more complex scope to grow, and thus, I had to find out a modified way to retain them by altering my product.

Eventually, both leader and the team members got prepared for every incoming client, for we all understood the market dynamics. We could segregate the market into different segments. One segment consisted of the early pickers who would try out every new thing whenever it reached the market. The second segment of customers waits for some time to indulge in something new, while the third type of customer needs a lot of validation.

Now, as an entrepreneur or a startup company, it was illogical for us to go to a customer falling under the third category because he/she would need time to experiment. Thus, we had to focus on that segment which was innovation-appreciator. As a leader, I couldn't simply push my team to crack a deal. Rather, I had to get into the fields to know the market status and then teach my team the right way to approach. As a leader, it was my job to analyze if the market was willing to have a trend-setter or was still conservative.

While putting my decades of experience into my pocket, I promise by John C. Maxwell's words – *Good leadership isn't about advancing yourself. It is about advancing your team.* I dispersed what I learned and also accumulated every ounce of knowledge from every corner. As a leader, it is often easy to make the rules clear and let the team understand the organizational goal and merge it with their personal ones.

However, we are humans, and our ideologies are bound to invite conflict. Businesses do not flourish under stagnant water. With new deals, changing demands, mergers, and acquisitions, many times organizational goals and performance barometers take a whole new avatar.

As a leader, one must keep a watch on the team's interest and inclination toward change. What if your high-performing team is not aligned with your company's goals? It is imperative to learn about your team members, their skills, intentions, and personal objectives before you lean on them as a leader. Delegating a task is just a small fraction of a leader's job; getting things done with the right spirit and full efficiency has a bigger room to occupy.

In today's business scenario, learning is about building a sustainable competitive advantage by building relationships, seeking valid information, making sense of observations, and sharing ideas through the intelligent use of new technologies. Leaders should embrace a lifelong learning strategy. It shall enable individuals to take control of their professional development through a continuous process of seeking, sense-making, and sharing while grabbing a personal mastery of knowledge.

A potential leader has to become a continuous seeker. In a world overflowing with information, we need smart filters to sort out the information that fits our pursuit. It requires us to evaluate and adjust the information sources on that we base our thinking and decision-making. It is necessary to be connected to a wise network of trusted individuals who can help us filter useful information, expose blind spots and open our eyes.

As a leader, you have to reflect upon your learning and put your knowledge. It involves critical thinking, where we weave together our thoughts, experiences, impressions, and feelings to make meaning of them.

On the same note, sharing includes exchanging resources, ideas, and experiences with the team. Sharing is a contributing process where we pass our knowledge forward, work alongside others, go through iterations, and collectively learn from important insights and reflections. There is no last page in the book of learning. There is no full stop in the process of learning. Also, there is no dearth of source of learning. It is a dynamic process, and the moment you try to make it static, you put an incessant pause in your growth curve. The more diverse your knowledge domain is, the more credible you become.

Unit 1

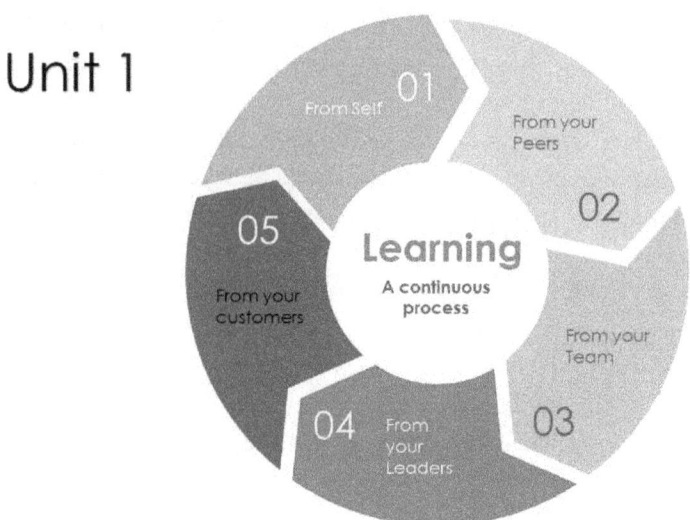

What You Must Learn on Your Own

As the saying goes —there is no better teacher than life; or what we can refer to as experiences. There are a few components of leadership that you have to learn or inculcate on your own.

- Observe your colleagues, peers, and everyone around you and extract their good qualities
- Work on your communication skills
- Learn something new from every interaction you encounter in a day
- Keep reading about the changing world
- Inculcate the habit of upskilling

Learning From Your Peers

Peer learning is one of the strongest ways to accelerate the employee development process. Discussing projects back and forth, explaining your perspectives, active listening, and refining an existing idea are some of the key benefits.

- Learning from your peers is called collaborative learning, which builds the premise of a stronger team.
- Essence of teamwork and collaboration.
- Sharing the joy of success and collaborative handling of failures.
- Building and accepting a strong and honest feedback loop.
- Gain newer perspectives.
- Career pathing.
- New hires speed quickly through peer-to-peer learning

Organizations also reap huge benefits by encouraging peer-to-peer learning through:

- Knowledge Sharing
- It is a cost-effective training
- Strengthens the company culture
- Fosters meaningful connections between employees

Things Only a Team Can Teach You

- No man is an island —You can never succeed alone
- Ability to put your personal desires aside for the greater good
- Taking ownership of your performance – good or bad
- Developing mutual trust
- Effective communication skills
- Planning and managing time and task
- Effective delegation of tasks by breaking them into parts.
- Ability to establish a shared identity.

What to Learn From Your Leader

A trusted leader can help you learn or have the following:

- You have a guide or sounding board for your ideas, helping you to decide the best course of action.
- Learning abilities and upskilling methods that can help you grow in the career graph.
- Effective persuasion and communication skills
- Learn a more advanced perspective.
- Network building abilities
- The art of tactful delegation
- The art of creating effective business strategies
- Managerial skills

Customers Are Not Only God but Teachers Too!!!

- Gain better insights of the changing market
- Honest feedback about your product and services
- Loopholes in your performance
- Better ideas to improve the product features
- Customers teach you to develop patience and hone your ability to remain calm.
- Improves your willingness to learn further and change.

"Continuous learning leads to continuous improvement. Commit yourself to advance your knowledge, skills, and expertise. The business environment is quickly changing, and your understanding of the leading practices, thinking, and emerging tools will help you manage for better results. Be a lifelong student."
— Pam Alabaster.

A Quick Fact Check

1. **What is there for a leader to learn?**

The right question is – what is NOT there to learn? Since the inception of the industrial revolution, there has not been a pause in development. Every new dawn began on a new note of change. So, when the world is changing, technology is evolving, and market dynamics are metamorphosing at a different pace altogether. A leader has more than enough on his/her plate to bridge the knowledge gap.

2. **I am the CEO. I don't see the need to learn anything new. I can delegate tasks to my subordinates.**

Ahem! And that is what I call as the biggest illusion one can have. It is the 21st century. People take orders from credible sources.
If you are not updated, you are outdated. Simple.

3. **I have built a great team. They can handle the tasks. Why should I poke my nose into it?**

Poking the nose is different from participating in the process. The more you indulge yourself in the daily affairs of your organization, the more you will be updated with the ground realities.

4. **I have strived for decades to attain this leadership role. When can I lean?**

Hmm! I would say, don't lean. You may take it slow but never lean because some or the other change or challenge is always there around the corner, and your team needs you to be able enough to guide them through.

The Little Birdie Knew It All

One of the most catastrophic economic shocks was The Great Depression, when unemployment climbed to 25% alongside a massive GDP drop. While most of the companies went ahead with the-board cuts to lower their overhead, Kellogg's took the opposite approach. The management doubled its advertising budget and re-invested in its workers shortly after the market crashed in late 1929. By 1933, Kellogg had increased its profits by 30% and distinguished itself as the USA's leading breakfast company. The company also innovated in its workforce. In order to create more jobs, the cereal manufacturer shifted to a 6-hour work day, giving workers a 12.5% raise in hourly wages while reducing working hours by 25%. Eighty-five percent of workers liked the 30-hour weekly schedule better, and worker productivity reached 40-hour levels within two years.

Kellogg's crisis strategy was successful because, at a time when other companies were making cuts, its increased advertising spending allowed its cereal brands to gain a greater share of consumer attention.

Also, the company's decision to invest in its workforce and the surrounding community developed a loyal, productive workforce that powered its success. These investments served as good publicity, with founder W.K. Kellogg earning an invite to the White House to discuss the 6-hour workday with President Herbert Hoover.

W.K. Kellogg proved that leadership must have a flexible rulebook, constantly innovating with unhindered learning.

Key Takeaways:

- Leaders cannot escape from continuous learning
- Every level in your career graph imparts a new lesson
- Learning should be all-embracing
- With continuous learning, leaders become the right fuel for the company's growth
- Shift focus from scalable efficiency to scalable learning
- Learning is about building a sustainable competitive advantage

2

CREDIBILITY IS AN OUTCOME OF CAPACITY

"Credibility is a leader's currency. With it, he or she is solvent; without it, he or she is bankrupt."

— John C. Maxwell

A learned man embodies confidence. With confidence and bountiful knowledge comes the element of conviction. With conviction, he builds concrete relationships. And as and when his actions churn out believable and profitable outcomes, he attains the Big C of Credibility. As continuous learning is inevitable for a leader, the more the leader learns, the more he widens his capacity to lead the team in the right direction. The more he widens his capacity, the better he gets a hold on market intelligence, customer demands, and satisfaction status, and also on the team's strengths and weaknesses.

Eventually, when a leader is bestowed with authority to chair a team, he is bound to get some respect by default. Some formal relationships take birth, and there will always be someone in the office to get the leader his favorite cappuccino.

However, does having someone getting your coffee equivalent to cracking a business deal? Or does it signify a leader's effective management skills? An organization has many components apart from its employees; investors, stakeholders, supply-chain section, and most importantly, the customers. As a leader, you can enjoy the authority to order your employee to get you a cup of coffee; however, you cannot treat your customers the same way. Neither can you do the same with your other stakeholders?

In the outer world, it is never your authority that fetches you the desired outcome. It is your credibility as a leader that can do the magic. Businesses run on the premise of the credibility of the organization, its leaders, and its products. Customers will buy your product if only your product is competitive enough to fulfill their needs. They will be drawn to a company whose top management is credible enough to run the show. The same happens with the investors and other stakeholders as well. A leader represents the company and thus is the designer of its image. Why do you think a TATA product is trusted blindly? It is not only because of the product but also for the grandeur image of Mr. Ratan Tata as a true-blue credible leader.

When we think about leaders' knowledge, very often, we find a particular aspect associated with it. Especially when knowledge bestows the person with an immense power to supervise or lead others, it often kindles the feeling of being a know-it-all, much like my previous story's old tribal leader. The power to lead is contagious and often infects the leaders with ego, so much so that they start considering themselves invincible. They tend to forget that effective management needs participation more than dictation from a singular voice.

With continuous learning, you can enhance your knowledge domain and capacity as a leader; probably enough to make a bunch of subordinates says YES-BOSS to your every utterance; however, business empires are not built through hollowed affirmations. A true leader must have a firm grip not only on his/her team's performance but also on the volatile situations of the market.

A leader's knowledge must be implementable in real-life scenarios to produce a visibly profitable outcome. Now, one of the critical questions that often make rounds while choosing an ideal leader is their educational background. Believe it or not, we all thrive within a validated misconception that a glorious degree can mold anyone into a great leader. However, is it true? There are highly qualified CEOs who have entered the Hall of Shame due to their misconduct and persistent disengagement with the day-to-day realities of the company.

Let's take some of the classic examples. Vikram Pandit, Citigroup's India-born chief, is proclaimed as one of the worst-ever CEOs in the all-time history of the corporate industry. A man who held an MBA and Ph.D. degree in Finance from the Columbia Business School and had a glorious two decades at Morgan Stanley was indeed considered to be someone at the top of his game. At the time he joined Citigroup, it was on track to report write-downs and increased credit costs of $20 billion. Although Pandit is not entirely responsible for the downturn of the company, he was found to be ill-equipped in commanding to save the firm.

Not to omit John Sculley. He let Steve Jobs go from Apple. Sculley was appointed as Apple's CEO in 1983, much like Google's board of directors selected Eric Schmidt to lead the firm with its young founders. Because of his extensive commercial expertise and marketing skills with the top post at PepsiCo, the board anticipated Sculley would bring a proven management style to Apple, as well as a mature business strategy to Apple, which was rapidly developing but was being led by inexperienced executives. Believe me, Steve Jobs was seen as an inexperienced executive.

In 1985, he persuaded the board to delegate all administrative authority to Jobs, thus sacking one of the greatest product designers and marketers of all time. Sculley believed in costly marketing initiatives; unfortunately, his marketing clout could not compensate for his lack of product management expertise. He lacked the technical knowledge required to be an Apple product manager.

During his tenure, he made significant investments in a variety of unsuccessful enterprises, including Apple's Newton, an early PDA-like gadget, cameras, and CD Players. Sculley's lack of technical abilities and understanding cost him his job in 1993.

Today, if you sit and surf the internet, you will find umpteen articles on CEOs who failed to prove their credibility as a leader even though they possessed prestigious degrees and glorious past experiences. A good pedigree indeed opens bigger doors of opportunities; however, it takes a lot more effort for leaders to prove their worth. A successful business can walk through every kind of water only when the leaders are capable of proving their credibility within and outside the organization.

Now, what is this credibility? In layman's language, credibility is defined as the quality of being accepted or believed as true, real, or honest. When we talk about personal credibility, it is about trust, respect, and being believable, while in an organizational context, a leader's credibility is ideally determined in terms of the degree of employee confidence, belief, and acceptance towards the leader. Much like how a leader must learn from different sources, the leader's credibility has to be proven to different segments of the business.

A leader must be credible enough for the team to follow his instructions and judgments. Similarly, he should prove his worth to the various stakeholders of the business, be they vendors, investors, or customers. No one would like to invest their time, money, and energy in a company that is not well-led.

Let's take a hypothetical situation to understand why this element of credibility is so crucial for effective leadership. Consider a situation of a business acquisition. Company XYZ has been a well-performing small-scale business that carries a promising future. A big conglomerate CBZ acquired it while retaining all its employees after considering their high proficiency and innovative style of working. In XYZ, the management strictly followed a participative style of leadership where every employee's concerns and ideas were entertained and encouraged as well.

On the other hand, CBZ's style was still orthodox, where every employee was given a set rule to follow and a job profile to perform. Initially, everything seemed good after the acquisition, as the core employees of XYZ got a chance to boast a big corporate tag on their resumes. However, they gradually felt the effect of change in their leadership style. All of a sudden, they were uprooted from any kind of collaboration with the top management.

Cocooned inside their designated cubicles, they found their voices and innovation snatched vehemently as the leader just designed and delegated the tasks without leaving any room for discussion. Moreover, it so happened that leaders took all the credit for the success and accused the team of the losses incurred. That is, all the good went to the higher-ups, while all the mishaps got attached to the actual performers. There prevailed many incidents when the employees could find the flaws in the system and still were not allowed to raise the issue lest the leader should be offended.

Eventually, that once-upon-a-time highly proficient team got trapped in a cage of mistrust and blocked their innovative mindset. They simply complied with the rule and remained reluctant to put efforts toward the ultimate organizational goal. Their morale was lowered by the so-called safe-playing leaders who would never want to get their hands dirty with the stark realities of the problems. Employees found their leaders not so credible enough to lead the organization, and slowly, they started walking out. In a couple of months' time, both the reputation and profitability of the company were impacted. The market was inundated with yet another news of a terrible business acquisition. At the same time, the job market received a bad reputation certificate for the big conglomerate.

Now, let me ask you the reason behind such a debacle. What would have gone wrong with XYZ's team? How could the same people perform differently under different leadership? We must understand that credibility has many facets. It is often judged mainly by comparing what one says with what one does in their day-to-day behavior. Today's market flourishes in the VUCA environment; volatility, uncertainty, complexity, and ambiguity.

Amidst such ever-changing and chaotic situations, leaders would lose their credibility and authenticity if they fail to stick to their own words. Being trustworthy isn't the only factor that contributes to your reputation as a leader.

People's trust in your expertise, talents, and capacity to do your job and get the job done as a leader are all crucial components of credibility. Employees create distinct opinions of their leaders not just via direct connection with them but also through the indirect observation of their behaviors and performance. And these views are critical in today's hyper-connected world when massive volumes of information about leaders are instantly accessible in the public domain. In the case of XYZ's inherent employees, they were initially shown a promising future; however, the new leaders could not match their expectations. Their performance declined because there was no alignment between their personal and organizational goals. The new leaders could never solve the persisting problems but had the audacity to blame the team for the failures.

A leader's credibility is important because employees want to have the assurance that when you are managing them and assessing their performance, you are competent enough to understand the ground realities prevailing in the market. Now, if you are chosen to be the leader, how can you self-assess your credibility in front of your team?

The process is simple. Ask a couple of questions like:

- Do your employees believe in your words and actions?
- Are they confident in your judgments?
- Do your employees believe that you have the overall organization's interest and employees' interests in mind while making strategic decisions?

If any of the aforementioned questions produce a 'no,' your credibility bridge needs some repair.

The present world is facing a myriad of challenges, from economic crisis to dreadful pandemic, and continues to face competitive and technological disruption.

Now, no business can prosper if the core team and the outside market fail to trust the assigned leader. There is a wonderful analogy prescribed by leadership scholars James Kouzes and Barry Posner — If you don't believe in the messenger, you won't believe the message. If an organization does not have credible leaders at the top layer, it cannot create a good rapport in the market. Similarly, if the leader is not competent enough to solve an issue for the team, his authority shall always remain under close scrutiny. It is a simple analogy. Why do we listen to our parents and teachers? It is because we find them knowledgeable enough to solve our day-to-day problems. Being a leader, if you cannot address routine affairs, you can never do a SWOT analysis of your organization.

Let me tell you about some of the factors that can actually undermine the leader's credibility both within and outside the organization.

Inaction and Indecisiveness

Leaders who fail to take appropriate actions at the time of crisis or have a tendency to ignore problems persisting in the system lose their credibility in front of the employees. Especially when it comes to problems that impact the sustainability of the organization, leaders' inaction poses a threat. One of the key roles of a leader is to make sense of the operating environment and make strategic decisions about the future of the organization. When you are seen as not fully clued into the operating environment and lack vision and clarity about the future direction of the organization, you quickly lose the respect of your employees. And once your employees cite the problems within you, your credibility hangs on a fine thread in the bigger market. John F. Akers, the then-CEO of IBM, has always been a great example of inaction.

During the mid-80s and 90s, when the rest of the world was moving toward personal computing, Akers failed to move ahead with the technological evolution. IBM was eventually paralyzed by his lack of indecisiveness.

Inconsistency and Faking Information

Many leaders are famous for making hollowed promises without making any effort to fulfill them. An inconsistent approach erodes credibility. Many leaders tend to over-promise, even if it is with good intentions, but at the time of real crisis, they shy away from putting their own hands in the dirt. When employees have accepted you as their leader, they would expect you to fulfill the commitments you have made to the team and the organization. Similarly, giving contradictory information confuses the team and lowers productivity. For example, Scott Thompson of Yahoo! was charged with adding up a fake computer science degree to his resume. He never needed a fake degree to embellish his credentials, but by the time the spotlight fell on him, he was too deep inside his web of lies.

> *"Perhaps the CEO's most important operational responsibility is designing and implementing the communication architecture for her company...Absent a well-designed communication architecture, information and ideas will stagnate, and your company will degenerate into a bad place to work...one-on-ones provide an excellent mechanism for information and ideas to flow up the organization and should be part of your design."*
> — Ben Horowitz

The leader's role is not limited to the walls of the organization. The different stakeholders of the company are also looking out for credible leaders. The investors or the key personnel of the supply-chain management need business leaders to be coherent with their communication and consistent with their credibility. When leaders create confusion among employees and other stakeholders by distributing incorrect or misleading information, or they misrepresent the facts, it can really undermine their credibility. Sometimes it is done without realization, and sometimes leaders do it intentionally to paint a rosier picture, to draw in more customers or investors. However, such dishonest attempts do not bear fruit for a long time.

Improper Communication

You can be a graduate of the Harvard Business School; however, your communication skills should be grounded enough to get things done from various stakeholders. Let's assume you are having a delivery issue. Can your business school certificate make your delivery department work properly? What if there is a problem happening in the whole supply-chain management section? Being the leader, you have to communicate with the right segment of the business to get things done. Can you just order and get things running smoothly? No. As a leader, you must be informed about the ground realities so that you can make informed communication. Every leader faces the Leadership Paradox, where the leader must know when to be rigid and when to be flexible.

A leader's personality type can be instructive enough to get things done. Soft personalities generally make poor managers because they need too much approval. Obsessives make better leaders as they are critical and cautious. Narcissists, on the other hand, are the closest to our common idea of great leaders because they have appealing, even gripping, plans for their organizations and the capacity to recruit followers. Remember Winston Churchill and his magnanimous speeches and action? However, even though their charisma can evoke action, narcissistic leaders are typically not comfortable to work with. Why? Because they listen only for the kind of exact information they seek. They don't learn easily from others and never prefer to teach but like to indoctrinate and make speeches. They dominate meetings with subordinates, which generates internal competition at a time when everyone is already under as much stress as they can take. The more successful the leader becomes, the more pronounced becomes the narcissist's faults.

Such an attitude may work within the organization but does not work well in the competitive market. A customer who is struggling to get his queries cleared will not need a boastful speech. Your vendors would want their payments cleared and not motivational messages.

Investors will be interested in your company only if you can showcase your effective planning and execution. Precisely, as a leader, your words should transcribe into profitable actions to create a win-win situation for both your organization and stakeholders.

Self-obsession Corrodes Credibility

Research shows that self-serving behavior can undermine employees' trust in their leaders. These include bending the rules to privilege yourself or your close associates, making decisions based on your self-interest rather than what's best for the organization, urging employees to make sacrifices while wasting the organization's resources on perks for yourself, and taking credit for the achievements of others. Even if you don't act yourself unethically, you can suffer a serious loss of trust if you permit colleagues to act unethically. You must uphold high ethical values to protect your organization, and your people, or your followers and key stakeholders will lose faith in you.

Carly Fiorina is a prime example of a high-profile CEO who is consumed with herself. She was the CEO of Hewlett-Packard from 1999 to 2005 and was a Sloan Fellow at the MIT Sloan School of Management. Her self-invested management had gone beyond all bounds when she lavished herself with incentives and privileges while laying off thousands of staff to save expenses. Her resume consists of more than 30,000 firings and a decline of 50 percent of the stock of the company. Her atrocity knew no limits when she urged employees to take voluntary pay cuts while outsourcing thousands of jobs overseas and thus causing huge layoffs.

Treating Staff and Stakeholders Poorly

Leaders who treat their employees as expendable or tend to openly ignore the opinions of employees and key stakeholders are perceived as untrustworthy and hence not credible. Leaders can damage their credibility when they ask for information and reports that don't seem worthwhile or that they don't review and act on. Such requests can cause confusion as to what the organization's priorities are, and the employees and other stakeholders may feel resentful about what they see as a waste of their time.

Are You Compromising on the Company's Value?

It is all about who you hire, who you fire, and who you promote. As a leader, what you reward and praise and what you condemn and correct make a whole lot of sense to your team as well as to the market as a whole. Why do you think Narayan Murthy had to make some tough calls after the firing-over-zoom fiasco?

As Rand Fishkin, founder of SEOmoz once quoted, *"If you're trying to figure out what a company's values really are, look at the decisions management makes when lots of money, risk, or loss of face for executives is at odds with the stated values. Want to know the company's mission & vision? Look at what they've intentionally chosen not to do, even though it could be lucrative."*

As a leader, your values must be a consistent part of how you lead. The picture you create for yourself is witnessed by your competitors in the market, your friends and foes, existing and potential customers, and also employees. If you cannot be firm with your values, your credibility is lost in the wilderness.

Are You Setting a Good Example?

An organization's foundation is built on its core culture. As a leader, you have to sow in the right ethics and culture that are implemented from the top to bottom level of your organization. Being the leader, you represent the company to the world and thus help in designing the market value of your company. When your actions reinforce what you say, you will be respected, and your team will act as you do. When you fail to set the right example, they will see you as a hypocrite, and you aren't likely to see the results you hope.

Now, credibility doesn't come to you as soon as you step into the shoes of leadership. Building credibility is a gradual process where you first build a rapport within the team and then proceed to the other stakeholders of the company.

Focus On Self-Organization First

Credibility is built by focusing on simple things rather than making things convoluted. You may be a high-profile management graduate with a great command over language; however, your staff is more competent in the technical aspect. If you keep delegating tasks in an incomprehensible manner, how can they implement your instructions? Impolite and arrogant dispersal of jobs never works out in this era. As a leader, you have to focus on transforming complex issues into a simple and understandable format for your team, vendors, and other stakeholders.

Secondly, self-organization also pinpoints your disciplined code of conduct. Just because you are the leader, you cannot take others' time for granted. Similarly, if you can locate any kind of knowledge gap within your team, you must make an effort to solve the issue. Your participation in providing solutions shall enhance your credibility as a leader. Focus on your attitude and mannerism. Arrogance never pays well in the market. Credibility is built by doing simple things in a disciplined manner without making things complex through arrogance.

Convince Over the Long-Term Success

It is different from making a strategic vision or setting performance targets and then just going about business as usual. It involves mapping out, in detail, how the organization will achieve its goals on a long-term basis. When employees get to see a clear picture through your confident perspective, they see a credible leader in you who has a clear mission in mind. As a leader, you prove your credibility as their true guide.

On the other hand, stakeholders also develop more faith in their abilities to lead the company. Having a sophisticated knowledge of industry trends and clear ideas about how the organization should respond to them build your credibility as a leader. You showcase yourself as capable enough to actively predict and prepare for upcoming changes. For example, if you make strategic investments in new technologies, you enhance your perceived competence.

Streamline Operations

When you work consistently to improve organizational structures and processes and maintain financially sound operations, your credibility as a leader soars. Eliminating unnecessary reporting structures and careless spending, establishing new strategic roles, or investing in technology that improves operational efficiency or business effectiveness shall tag you as an action-oriented and competent leader.

Be Vigilant

As a leader, you must always look out for stakeholders' needs. This way, you can prevent stakeholder conflicts and organizational crises, as well as gain the trust of your employees and other key stakeholders. As you sit at the top level of the hierarchy, you cannot remain myopic. Your vision should be streaming down the pyramid, and at every stage, you have to prove your worth.

Be it with the technical team, administrative wing, PR, or with customer care section. In fact, we are all aware of situations when a customer's problem does not get resolved by the designated employee.

And eventually, the leader has to intervene. Now, what if the leader is unaware of the solution and blatantly reveals his inability? His credibility is lost in front of his team and customers as well. So, is it like, the leader should always be ready with the solution? No, not possible.

However, as an efficient communicator, the leader can convince the customer to retain the services and can showcase his enthusiasm to the staff by participating in the process of solution providers.

Be the Role Model

Be clear about your values and the organization's values so that employees and other stakeholders can see why you do what you do. The culture of the organization flows from the top. If you want your employees to trust you, you need to start by showing that you trust them. If you want your employees to be open to change, be change-ready yourself. Basically, know that your employees are observing you minutely all the time, and if you want them to behave in a certain way, they need to see you doing the same. Demonstrate your values in how you talk and act to establish credibility and authenticity as a leader.

> *"Before you are a leader, success is all about growing yourself. When you become a leader, success is all about growing others."*
> — Jack Welch

Your success as a leader and the success of your organization depends on your credibility. It takes time to build, but it can be torn down in seconds. Not every leader needs a scandalous hoarding roaring all over the internet to lose their credibility. It is often the little things that you do over time that can add up to destroy your credibility.

Have you ever observed the organizational skill of ants? A lot can be learned from the way ants do their jobs. The right ants in the right jobs. Everyone counts. Ants do not differentiate between excellent and terrible performers. They just assign the appropriate ants to the appropriate duties. The strong are designated as warriors, while the smaller ones look after the newborns. The medium-sized ones become employees.

If any new ants from other colonies attempt to join in, they are promptly detected as "the wrong individuals in the wrong positions" and eliminated. Now, can humans not do the same? If a person doesn't perform well, he can be put on a task that he can do well. There is no point in criticizing him. However, as a leader, if you can't find the right job for the person, remove him. People cannot be kept only for the sake of retaining them. If you do decide to maintain them, make sure that what they do is meaningful and that everyone in the organization understands that.

Ants are highly social creatures. If one discovers food, it will alert the others. If there is a threat, warrior ants are alerted. If the queen requires assistance in caring for her children, her devoted servants will appear instantly. This extremely efficient machine operates on the basis of continual, direct, and truthful communication. Leaders may do the same thing. Bring people together, ask them to make a choice, eliminate strong voices, and emphasize that everyone's viewpoint matters; fruitful foster talks, and the entire business will benefit.

Do you know that all ants will have a common intent? They all want to survive. Let me ask a very vital question; why do we work? To earn a living. But to survive within an organization, we have to fulfill the organizational goal before making any personal gains. As a leader, you must communicate the common intent to the whole team. It's the leaders' duty to make sure that the vision is right and that the team has the appropriate tools to execute the plan.

Ants are highly adaptable. They can easily switch from one source of food to another as and when the situation demands. If one source of food turns poisonous for the colony, they will soon change direction. A credible leader should also be flexible enough to embrace the new wave of change. Ants are firm believers in teamwork. Ants focus more on the needs of the colony than their own individual needs. As a leader or an employee, concentrating on self can be detrimental to the overall performance of the team or the entire organization.

Research has proven that ants take care of others' babies only because it is the right thing to do. Process ownership and doing the right thing are essential to becoming a credible leader. Ants are accountable for their actions. A leader's credibility is proven when he takes charge to do the right thing. By doing the right thing, humans can increase their own performance and the level of customer service they deliver.

Why? Because they care about the deliverable, not themselves! Also, ants perform peer reviews all the time. They constantly smell each other to see if they belong to the colony. They teach each other to work and hold each other accountable. Providing peer review and holding team members accountable is what brings performance to the team. If you don't comply, you are out! Sometimes, leaders do have to make the nastier decisions for the better good.

So, what is the bottom line? Leaders can improve their organizations by focusing on overall performance. They should establish and agree on strategic intent, create a system of peer-based checks and balances, socialize for performance, and accept the constantly changing environment. The leader's credibility is enhanced when he is able to create a culture of people that lead themselves and create a team environment that reduces mistakes and ensures success. Research has shown that 75 percent of people leave their bosses and not their companies. Poor leadership has a huge impact on the workforce. As a matter of fact, the job of a leader is to get out of his people's way.

> *"To remain a credible leader, I must always work first, hardest, and longest on changing myself. This is neither easy nor natural, but it is essential."*
> — John C. Maxwell

A Quick Fact Check

1. Am I not authorized to order my staff?

Of course, yes. As a leader, you can order your staff. But are you capable enough to do it yourself before ordering your staff to do the task? What if they get stuck somewhere in between? Will you be able to resolve the issue?

2. Is Leadership Paradox a myth?

Not at all. A leader's life is not a bed of roses. He has to have both carrot and stick by his side. Leadership is the right blend of rigidity and flexibility. Leaders must be flexible to change with time while being rigid enough with the organization's vision.

3. How can I make my team trust my abilities?

Simple. Make your actions speak louder than words. Participate in the process. Always choose encouragement over criticism. Dig deeper into the problems and provide solutions, and always remain a learner.

4. How can I improve my image as a leader?

Introspect. Leaders are not infallible. Seek feedback from your peers, subordinates, and other stakeholders and mend the gaps.

A Leader Who Never Failed To Impress

APJ Abdul Kalam was known as the People's President and served our country in that capacity from 2002 to 2007. His idea was for India to achieve nuclear prominence in the global arena. India's Missile Man is well-known for his contributions to the development of ballistic missiles and space rocket technologies.

His journey from newspaper kid to President of India is inspiring, particularly because of his determination to face life's challenges. The SLV-3 was Dr. A.P.J. Abdul Kalam's first significant project at ISRO in 1979. It was a colossal flop. As a team leader, he said, "When failure occurred, the leader of the organization owned that failure. When success came, he gave it to his team. The best management lesson I have learned did not come to me from reading a book; it came from that experience." He re-launched the SLV-3 a year later, in 1980. And it was a smashing success. He was elected President of India in 2002, with the backing of both the government and opposition parties, and ruled until 2007. As a leader, his clear vision, drive, and humility made him an extraordinary human being for the entire globe.

Key Takeaways:

- Businesses run on the premise of the credibility of the organization, its leaders, and its products
- A good pedigree is not enough to prove a leader's worth
- With no credible leaders at the top layer, no organization can create a good rapport in the market.
- Inaction, indecisiveness, and improper communication corrodes credibility
- Building credibility is a gradual process.

3

DIRECTING AND DOING
The Two Eyes of Leadership

Have you ever wondered how it would be if we had only one eye? Or just consider someone lacking vision in one of the two eyes. Scientifically, apart from imparting a beautiful symmetry to our faces, the two eyes help us see the world in three dimensions. We can analyze the depth and distance accurately because of the positioning of our eyes. Both eyes perceive the image of an object at different angles, and then the image is registered on the retina. The brain receives the final two images and starts processing them. Once the processing is done, a three-dimensional aspect is obtained, which enables us to experience the length, width, and height of the object. With my few decades of experience, I have always found the dire need to have two such eyes for nurturing an effective leadership standard.

In the corporate world, it is a spiral staircase to reach the pinnacle, convoluted steps, and you must keep a steady balance with each step you take forward. Have you ever reached the top of a spiral staircase and tried to look down? It looks serpentine, and at every angle, your view is blocked with a large curvature.

Consider this staircase as your organizational hierarchy, with each protrusion representing a department. Now, as your view tries to penetrate deeper, your vision is partially blocked by the curvatures at the top. You can hardly see what is happening at the bottom. What should you do to have a clear picture? Either you should have someone placed at the other end to communicate every happening authentically, or you should make an attempt to go down periodically to have a hands-on experience.

It so happens that when someone reaches the pinnacle of top management, they relax on the couch of their past experience, success stories, and failed attempts and eventually become stagnant in their approach to handling things. Their past failures make them hesitant to take certain risks, while with their success history, they try to make it universal. Why? Because humans are inherently lazy, reluctant to accept change, and prone to settle down easily. After putting years of hardwork into their self-growth and training the team, leaders often tend to take the sole responsibility of directing and delegating. Eventually, they turn a blind eye to acting.

Now, imagine a traffic controller wearing a bandit eye patch. With one eye open, he can see only one portion of the road and can keep on directing them while the other side is not entertained at all. What will happen? On the other side, traffic will be halted, and people will be miffed by the traffic controller's inaction.

Action and direction are two eyes for maintaining effective leadership in any organization. As a leader continues to learn, he widens his knowledge domain so much so that he can fathom everything, even if that goes beyond his core competency. For example, a salesman who climbed the ladder of success to become the leader of his company is now well-versed in every segment of the company, from product design to customer issues. But what if he feels that he has a great team to handle the day-to-day affair, and he should take a backseat? Possible enough. In such cases, the highly efficient team does perform its role efficiently but for a short duration of time.

Why? Because it is a VUCA market—volatile, uncertain, complex, and ambiguous. And it shall remain so forever because change is the only constant. Every day the world is shifting to a new dimension. Whether it is a technological disruption or a change in customer needs, every organization is facing a new wave of change. What knowledge and skills were valid yesterday may not remain viable in the future. So as a leader, you can never settle on anything but your core organizational culture and ethics. That is, if your ultimate objective is to have customer satisfaction, you need not change that; however, with time, as the customer needs change, the process of customer retention and attaining customer satisfaction should be modified.

As a leader, if you sit at the top without learning about the changing environment, how can you decipher the need for new skills to be incorporated into the team? If you don't grasp the changing demands, you cannot implement a solution. Similarly, if you simply direct and do not get involved and take any action in the process of restructuring and refining, your own knowledge and skills remain limited. After all, at the end of the day, a leader cannot simply say that I lead a team of marvelous coders without having an iota of knowledge about coding.

The moment you forget to take action and focus on directing alone, you uncheck your credibility as a leader. My initial days in the Edtech sector were more like working in solitude. I used to have direct interaction with all my clients; however, as and when my team grew in number, I could curtail my direct interactions with the clients. Still, I always had a few exclusive clients within my reach. Although I was leading a team and I could delegate many of my jobs to my well-trained team, I kept a thorough touch with a few of my clients so that I didn't lose control over our overall product and performance. It so happened once that one of my clients faced an issue and contacted me to resolve it. As I went through the problem, I realized its possibility to happen with my other customers as well. I resolved the issue and upskilled my team about the impending problem and its solution.

Also, I took the initiative and informed myself about the probability of such a problem to my other clients. In fact, I urged them to communicate with us directly as and when such occurrences happen. As my personal experience reveals, this one particular incident made me a hero not only in front of my esteemed clients but also in my team.

As a leader, when I was informed about a problem, I did not delegate the problem to my team. Rather I worked out a solution along with my team to resolve the issues for my customers. While I looked for the solution, I could find the knowledge gap and could bridge them for future reference and help my team. In turn, my respect as their leader was enhanced, and soon, the customer market knew me as someone to be an action-packed leader. The whole situation gave me one important lesson in life. The more a leader keeps himself grounded with the realities of the market, the more he will be able to innovate. And the moment he gets cocooned inside the power of direction and delegation, his innovative mindset will enter into hibernation.

Let's take a hypothetical case scenario to understand the correlation between action-oriented leadership and innovation. While working a 9-5 corporate job, Mr. ABC weaved an innovative idea with his knowledge and acquired skills and decided to venture into the world of entrepreneurship. The product was innovative and gained momentum quickly. Soon, Mr. ABC grabbed all the eyeballs, and his business flourished.

Eventually, Mr. ABC decided to take control of the financial aspects of the business and left the product and customer department completely in the hands of his team. The clock kept ticking; a few problems cropped up with the product, but Mr. ABC delegated the team to sort out the issue. The team did try, and some of the problems got sorted out, too; however, a few didn't work out. Considering ABC's reluctance to get his hands on the problem, the team decided to hide the information from him. The scenario changed, and in a couple of years, a new player came into the market with a more advanced version of ABC's product.

This new version could rectify all the issues that were associated with ABC's product. It was a terrible shock that once a successful entrepreneur was outcompeted by a newcomer in a matter of few months. While digging deeper, ABC found that he was always kept in the dark because he projected himself as a mere director. His product design and customer relation team could never contact him for any suggestions. Even if they tried, the matter got lost in the web of hierarchy.

So, do I oppose the hierarchy in organizational management? Not exactly. In this case, no one person can be blamed for the loss. When a leader remains far from getting into action, the team eventually loses interest in communicating the problem. There prevails mistrust within the team and the management. Additionally, as the information flows through the line of hierarchy, it is bound to get diluted. Even if ABC was aware of the problem, he wouldn't have known the magnitude because, at every stage, the message got filtered. Why? Sometimes it is due to different interpretations by different people, while many times, the team has not communicated the exact situation out of fear—what if you are sacked?

In ABC's case, as the product went to the dungeon, Mr. ABC took a closer look at the problems. Was it unsolvable for him? Never. All he needed was the right information to innovate further and upgrade his product. As he relaxed on his action, he lost touch with his own product, and his innovation cycle stopped. He got so engrossed in the other aspects of the business that he literally lost connection with the market demands and the scope of improvement for his own product.

As a leader, it is essential to remain in action to keep the innovation cycle moving. When you become a leader, it is obvious that you have at least achieved 80% of what the organization needs out of you. As days pass by, new challenges crop up. And if you remain active in the field, you get first-hand experience in designing a new solution. Thus, the more action you take, the more skilled you become and the more trust you garner from your team.

But then there is a hitch. A leader should not become over-conscious in providing a solution all the time. Whenever a leader starts taking every action on behalf of his team, there are two possible consequences. The team may become too reluctant to think and innovate as they are assured that the job will be done by the leader. They will just become a puppet and will never take any responsibility on their shoulder. In another scenario, the whole team may nurture a kind of distrust as they presume the leader is not trusting their abilities at all.

In short, it is about having the right balance between action and direction. When a leader goes out of the way to solve an organizational issue, he indirectly prevents the next in the hierarchy from learning the ground realities of struggle and winning over the hurdles. A leader's role is to guide in the right direction by taking suitable action while preparing the team for the future course of action.

> *"If your actions inspire others to dream more, learn more, do more, and become more, you are a leader."*
> —John Quincy Adams

Leadership is not about seniority but about providing guidance, motivation, and clarity and inspiring confidence among your juniors and peers. How a leader's actions impact the team, and the overall organization is highly determined by the leadership style. In fact, in today's fast-paced world, no one style of leadership can fulfill the needs of the changing scenarios.

It is true that some leaders are born; however, leadership is a continuous learning process in itself. It is imperative to understand the blurring line between leadership and management. A manager provides direction, while a leader must inspire the whole organization through his knowledge, action, and power of delegation. Over the years, businesses have evolved, and so is the leadership style, which went beyond autocratic, democratic, and laissez-faire styles.

Transformational leadership has found a prominent place in today's organizations. When I urge budding leaders to incorporate a balance between action and direction, it is obvious for them to understand the basic rules of different leadership styles. The world is full of inspiring leaders who could script pages of history in gold. For example, Margaret Thatcher was the longest-serving British Prime Minister and was well-known for her autocratic leadership style. Often quoted as Iron Lady, she led the British into the Falklands War, battled against the nation's then-powerful trade unions, and privatized many of the country's state-owned organizations. On the other hand, Larry Page introduced his transformational and democratic leadership style and kept himself always open to ideas developed by his employees.

Peter Drucker once said, *"Leadership is lifting a person's vision to higher sights, the raising of a person's performance to a higher standard, the building of a personality beyond its normal limitations."* Now, internal and external circumstances play a vital role in deciphering the style of leadership the company needs. Steve Jobs encouraged a collaborative style of working, but he was also a 'get-it-done' kind of leader as and when the situation demanded.

There are times when a leader must incorporate an autocratic style and instruct the team to do as told. In such scenarios, direction comes from the top, and a singular figure leads a company or team. An autocratic leader determines strategy, policies, procedures, and the direction of the organization and dictates everything to subordinates.

Autocratic leaders often possess qualities like decisiveness, self-confidence, and focused commitment to the goal, and inevitably, such qualities are always inspirational for the subordinates. Autocratic Leadership, or this 'Don't question my actions and commands' approach, although doesn't sound very acceptive; however, becomes essential during urgent or chaotic situations that require someone to lead the team and make a prompt and effective decision.

Treading on the same note, employees working under an autocratic leader often feel micromanaged, as the leader remains the sole decision-maker. The thinking potential and innovation cycle of the employee are paralyzed under such a leadership style.

As the world is getting disrupted every now and then with technological evolution, participation and innovation must become a constant companion for a leader. In the democratic style of leadership, although the leader remains the ultimate decision maker, the subordinates or the team are allowed to participate in the process of identifying and solving a crisis. It is often found that democratic leaders excel at sparking creativity among subordinates, and the final outcome is always enhanced when positive contributions come from all sides. Microsoft Corporation co-founder Bill Gates, Nelson Mandela, and

Walt Disney, President of The Walt Disney Company, are some of the best-known democratic leaders.

However, not every leader or every situation can have success with the democratic approach. Inevitably, there will be employees who feel left out because their ideas or solutions were not chosen. Further, what if the leader places confidence in the group to theorize solutions when the group is not skilled or trained to answer the call?

In my case, I had to incorporate different styles of leadership in different situations. As I paced up in the Edtech sector, my team had encounters with different kinds of clients. There were deals that were tough to break, clients who never entertained any negotiation, and then there were times when the process felt as smooth as a feather. Now, as a leader, I had to tread carefully on the path of action and direction.

The moment I fathomed that a deal could be cracked easily by my area manager himself, I never invested my time into that project. Rather, I gave the full liberty to the team to go ahead and take a call that they deemed fit for the whole organization. However, in the case of tough clients where I could see repeated failure to accomplish the deal, I intervened and took necessary actions to convince the client. Eventually, I had to switch to an autocratic mode of conduct and just directed the team with tailor-made solutions.

In any business environment, challenges hone the creative instinct. Every tough client showed me a new way to chalk out a better plan which I could later teach to my team. As a leader, I had to analyze the client, the market situation, the competitive edge, and my team's potential. An out-of-the-box demand made me think twice about a solution and helped me to upskill myself as well as my team. And once I could highlight the tough clients and critical situations, I was able to empower my team well enough to trust them to accomplish the task at hand. Eventually, I did get opportunities to enjoy a Laissez-faire style of leadership too.

'Who Cares' is a misconception that hovers around the Laissez-faire style. Laissez-faire leaders are excellent at delegating and also instill confidence in employees while assigning them tasks without oversight. They provide constructive criticism when needed and are often seen as trusting, as they willingly place responsibilities in the hands of employees. In my personal space, I have found, it often leads to faster decision-making as the employees are trained well and don't require supervision. However, hands-off can be problematic when if the team doesn't fully understand the mission. Unless the leader has complete confidence in the employees and their collective ability to complete a task without close supervision, the laissez-faire approach needs to be reconsidered.

While growing a business, the leader has two options to go ahead with the flow of change. Either the leader fits in and lets the world accommodate his style of working, or the leader may choose to stand out and let the world reward him. And this idea of standing out needs a lot of innovation, where every day, the leader and the whole team must transform and evolve, both personally and professionally. A transformational leader is the need of the hour as constant evolution and innovation have become the new norm. Such leadership style understands the very essence of change, the need, and its probable outcome and, in turn, encourages participation from the team. In such scenarios, the leader shows the right path of execution through productive actions.

In the bestselling book *Outliers,* the 'pop economist' Malcolm Gladwell says, *"Practice isn't the thing you do once you are good. It's the thing that makes you good."* In a constantly evolving world, an action-oriented leader guides a vision forward with a team to reach objectives and make progress.

However, there obviously prevails a constant change in priorities and a dynamic work environment, and it becomes challenging for the leaders to keep a watch on the productivity of the team. The leader must think in terms of the team as a whole and focus on both individual and collective progress because successful teamwork requires both individual and collective awareness. When we think about action-packed leadership, it is about ensuring constant learning with hands-on experience. A leader must keep on practicing to make him more and more credible in front of the team as well as the market.

There are seven crucial elements attached to the action-oriented leadership style. Let's have a look at them.

What is your vision?

A leader who intends to act successfully must have a strong foundation; a vision that provides clarity about the mission and how to accomplish the task at hand. It is a collective understanding as the team must follow the same vision as its leader. Vision is the first essential factor that any leader should have clarity about and be able to articulate to the team.

How supportive are you as a leader?

An organization works with a team which is more like a system with different components attached to it. And like any other system, every component must work in cohesion to accomplish an objective. A leader who is too indulged in action or direction often overlooks the support system the human component of the organization needs.

It is a leader's duty to support the team to ensure engagement, high morale, and retention. Important aspects of team dynamics happen on the individual level. Each team member needs different versions of support that come in the form of environment, mentorship, and schedule preferences that fuel their best work.

Defining every role accurately

It is imperative to define every employee's role in the organization. Along with a clear vision, the leader must break the structure into who is supposed to do what and up to what extent. Defining the role includes individual understanding in terms of specific responsibilities — which actions fall under which person's responsibility on the team. Teams that don't have proper roles defined work in different directions and feel confused and never get to know when to call for external support. Let's assume the case of dealing with a difficult client. The assigned salesman has limited capacity and authority to decide on certain crucial factors, and once he is clear with his role and limitations, he can seek timely intervention from his leader.

What resources are you providing to your team?

The systems and equipment that your team uses regularly are like extensions of your abilities. An action-oriented leader must focus not only on his own upskilling but also on his team's skill levels. The more time a leader spends on optimizing the organization's resources, the better becomes the team's performance. A leader's action-oriented game plan involves working with the team to make sure they have the resources they need to put their best foot.

A leader's action is defined by context

Context is the understanding of the landscape of the organization beyond your team's immediate work scope. Without understanding the context beyond the immediate team environment, teams work in silos which eventually makes the job inapplicable to the larger mission of the organization. With a big-picture understanding of the company's mission and goals, knowledge of the company landscape, and understanding of people and operations within the company, team members appreciate and understand the true utility and value of their work. As a leader, instead of directing which way to go, act diligently by educating the team in the right direction. Taking action is not always about providing a readymade solution to the team; however, it is more about empowering the whole team about the impending challenges.

A leader's action should motivate others

In the heat of the day-to-day pressure to get things done, action-oriented leaders very often indulge in solving the problem on their own without motivating the employees to think and innovate a solution. In a dearth of appreciation and motivation to become a problem-solver, the team and the leader hatch an environment of animosity and disconnection.

Freedom is the key element

Is it about taking a complete break from the action? No. An action-oriented leader does the groundwork for the whole team to learn and grow in the future. The element of freedom is not from the action but from the constant scrutiny of the team's performance. As the leader shows the path by acting suitably, he ensures that the team is now equipped enough to deal with similar problems. Leaders that work toward freedom and achieve it in their work lead with authenticity, dedication, and alignment.

While you work on these vitals, you have to ponder upon some critical questions:

- Where is the root of your challenges?
- Is your team clear with the vision and strategy to follow?
- As a leader, have you provided enough resources and support to your team to accomplish the assigned task?
- Is your action speaking louder than your words?

These questions form the navigation system of an action-oriented leader and aid in complete awareness, which in turn, cultivates clarity and creates aligned and effective action. As a leader, the first action is to identify which vital is imbalanced and where you need to focus on to align and motivate your team. Eventually, the seven vitals and exercises for clarity and creativity will bring out some of the authentic leadership qualities necessary to lead a team successfully. In the spiral staircase of corporate growth, a leader's action and authenticity are more crucial than his authority.

Let's take this hypothetical case scenario to understand an employee's reaction to witnessing a proactive leader. As the financial year was approaching an end, the accounts manager was doing some rigorous auditing. During late working hours, he could find a wide gap in the books and planned to discuss it with the leader the very next day. The new dawn came up with a surprise when the leader himself made a call and provided a couple of suggestions to rectify the issue. The accounts manager was newly appointed and never expected a leader to know the minutia of such a problem, that too when the leader is not from the finance background. However, the leader's informed suggestions built an inerasable note of credibility in this accounts manager's mind. He now knew that the organization was certainly on the right path of progress.

But what if an otherwise proactive leader becomes inactive while climbing the ladder of success? Can it happen? Of course. I have faced huge repercussions while underestimating the concept of information dilution. The more I went to the next level of the hierarchy, the lesser I became the direct contact of communication. If earlier, I could get information from forty members of the organization, slowly, it became four.

There happened a situation when a customer was dissatisfied. I did get the information but never the magnitude, as the information was diluted in each step. Moreover, by the time I could get the full picture, the customer was out of my reach. It was a huge lesson of inaction I could learn in my leadership role. I realized that even if I am at the top of the hierarchy, I must learn the customer needs on a daily basis. Since then, whenever I plan for a pilot project, my first set of feedback provider remains my clients. I always keep in touch with my four to five key clients and seek their honest feedback before implementing anything new in the market.

Why? Because the team will anyway work on the guidelines, while the critical question is, will the customer accept the guideline? The real challenge in today's world is to please the ever-changing needs of the customer base. As technology revolutionizes, the market needs keep fluctuating, and the leader's role grows beyond the scope of directing a bunch of efficient people. Over a period of time, even the highest performing team can lose the sheen if not constantly kept abreast with the newer developments. And at the end of the day, it is the leaders' role to take all the necessary action to keep the organization growing.

On the same note, being action-oriented has more to do beyond the scope of a particular leadership style. A leader must make a balance between three core elements of the organizational goal — Task, Team, and Individual. While task refers to the action the leader takes to achieve the goal, the team refers to the action the leader takes to encourage the right people at the right job, and the individual refers to the leader's action in supervising the individual needs of the performing team. In practice, achieving a balance between these three components is not easy. You may face intense pressure to hit sales or production targets. But if you prioritize the task at the expense of the team and the individuals who are working hard to achieve it, problems can arise in those neglected areas. Let's say that your team works well together, but one person is falling behind schedule. And thus, productivity declines, the team misses its deadline, and group morale suffers.

In this case, an individual's flaw negatively impacts the task and the team. On the other hand, imagine what would happen if you, as a leader, didn't clearly state your team's goal. Your team members are highly skilled, and they collaborate well, but progress is slow because no one knows what they're aiming for. In this example, individual and team needs are being met, but the task itself is being ignored, and the team is likely heading for failure. So, essentially, an action-oriented leader has to develop the individual, achieve the task and also build an effective team.

The real-world demands of leadership will never let you balance your efforts across every domain of leadership. Every new situation would ask for a new strategy. When all three areas of responsibility compete for your attention, you will have to prioritize. Start by considering your organization's goals. But then there may be times when the customers' needs may want you to change. A true-blue leader always uses his prudence to decide what balance of responsibilities works best at that point in time and adjust the focus accordingly. The key is to limit the change in focus to the short term and to restore the balance when the matter is resolved.

> *"Leadership is about making others better as a result of your presence and making sure that impact lasts in your absence."*
> — Sheryl Sandberg

A Quick Fact Check

1. **I am exhausted from being in action for so long. What should I do?**

Becoming an action-oriented leader is not equivalent to doing every single task in the organization. Empowering your team to be self-reliant is the biggest action a leader must take.

2. **Am I supposed to switch between action and direction?**

There is no set time to suit yourself into these two roles, much like how it is natural for us to see through both eyes; action and direction are simultaneous processes. If direction ensures your authority, continued action widens your grasp of ground realities and builds on your credibility.

3. **My team seems to be relaxed about seeing me in action. What should I do?**

Never tailor-make a solution for your team. Encourage participation and become a transformational leader to ensure the team knows the nitty-gritty of the challenge and the probable solution.

4. **The problem is beyond my skillset; I cannot act. But I have a team to work on it. I can delegate, right?**

Technically yes. But how long can you justify this? You need not become a master in that particular skill, but you can always work with your team and learn about the problem and how the solution can build a better business. No?

5. **What is the problem if I prefer being blindfolded?**

Eventually, you become outdated, and no one respects an outdated leader for sure.

An Interaction worth a Read

In March 2022, Narayana Murthy, Founder-Infosys, addressed CEO's, MDs, and many senior leaders from ETILC regarding the significance of leadership in the current challenging times. Madhav Thapar, Vice President - South Asia, Middle East & Africa, C.H. Robinson, posed a wonderful question about the changing work environment as the ongoing virtual work has been refurbishing the work-from-anywhere style.

Mr. Narayana Murthy provided five key points as the following:

- *Achieve respect from every stakeholder; be it a customer, employee, investor, the government of the land, or the society as a whole. If we earn respect, customers, employees, investors, and suppliers will trust us as credible leaders and would want to repeat business.*
- *Leaders must walk to talk and practice the precept to build credibility for their words.*
- *Competition remains the best management guru.*
- *Performance is the only instrument that all leaders, not just corporate leaders, have at their disposal to earn the respect of their stakeholders. The past is dead, so there is no point in claiming the past success stories. Similarly, the future is uncertain, and the only thing that matters is performance in the present.*
- *There is no substitute for meritocracy, hard work, teamwork, honesty, transparency, and accountability. A leader has to let go of the ego and must learn from people who have performed better.*

Key Takeaways:

- Action and direction are two eyes for maintaining effective leadership in any organization
- Forgetting to act uncheck your credibility
- Leadership styles determine the impact of leader's actions on the team, and on the overall organization
- Empowering your team to be self-reliant is the biggest action a leader must take
- Taking action is not about tailor-making the solutions

PART 2

LETTING THE ANTHILL GROW

4

ACTIONS SPEAK LOUDER THAN ANECDOTES

Are you aware of any brand that is famous for NOT ADVERTISING? Ridiculous! Amidst this throat-choking competitive world, how can a brand even survive without being loud about its products? But then, there is a brand. A famous one is more famous for its actions being louder than words or advertising (to sound more accurate). Tesla.

Elon Musk's Tesla does not seem to be very fond of advertising; nevertheless, it has transformed itself into one of the most compelling brands of the past few decades. Now, there could be many reasons, be it an outspoken CEO or a market-leading products chief.

However, my opinion is reserved for their biggest quality — they don't just TALK big while reflecting upon their purpose. They take big and bold ACTIONS too. In fact, there were situations when some of their actions became a serious risk of undermining their market position.

In this competitive market, it is indeed crucial for every brand to set and stick relentlessly to an economical yet progressive and aspirational brand value that can instigate a larger impact.

In 2019, when Elon Musk tweeted about his unprecedented step of releasing Tesla's patents for universal use, his action spoke louder than the stated purpose of the company.

In Musk's own words – *"The overarching purpose of Tesla Motors is to help expedite the move from a mine-and-burn hydrocarbon economy towards a solar electric economy."*

Tesla believes that its competition is not with the non-Tesla electric vehicles but with the enormous number of petrol/diesel-run vehicles pouring out into the market every day. It was a bold (sometimes terrifying) decision to make your patents available to everyone. However, Musk was clear in his purpose; that is, better availability of technology will lead to more compelling electric vehicles and less reliance on hydrocarbons.

If you think wisely, Musk's step is to widen the niche of electric vehicle technology. Now, how many brands or present-day leaders have such a big and bold-sounding purpose? Even if they have, the purpose is undermined by actions to appease the different stakeholders of the business. As a leader, if your words sound hollow and never get accentuated by your actions, you can never build trust amongst your team members.

Consider a situation when you motivate your team to work toward a particular goal but fail to appreciate their efforts as the new investor has asked for a different plan altogether, and you go with the investor's goal. Consider a situation when you keep talking about gender equality and pay parity but invariably remain biased while delegating important tasks to your team.

A similar ambiguity can arise even in the customer market. What if you make a dishonest proclamation about your products? There are cases where leaders' arrogance has slaughtered the whole reputation of the company. McDonald's Steve Easterbrook failed to recognize the essentiality of company ethics and permanently damaged the company's reputation.

Similarly, Richard Smith of Equifax is accused of improper assimilation of customer data which led to 143 million people's personal and financial data. In 2019, Musk's step appeared like a big gamble. But eventually, it seemed like an inspired action to elevate the brand value.

As you grab the role of leadership, take a closer look at your company, team, and all the concentric circles of glory and failures. And ponder upon one thing – how aligned is your word with actions? Are your decisions actually sticking to the loud anecdotes you produce? Do you take concrete actions that advance your business? If the answer to either of these questions is no, then, believe me, your qualification and credibility as a leader is diminished.

You have been making some empty promises, not only within the walls of your organization but also in the outer market. Your team, peers, subordinates, other stakeholders, and also the customers want to see your present course of action without having much admiration for your past achievements.

> *"Leadership is not about a title or a designation. It's about impact, influence, and inspiration. Impact involves getting results, influence is about spreading the passion you have for your work, and you have to inspire team-mates and customers."*
> — Robin Sharma

The world has witnessed a myriad of leadership styles. While some leaders could remain immortal in the pages of history, some scratched the floor for their unethical and unsuitable code of conduct. Adolf Hitler was a great orator and plausibly could transform each uttered word into action, irrespective of the final outcome.

Still, the world does not worship him as a great leader. Why? Because his actions never translated into a greater good. When I urge leaders to make their actions louder than anecdotes, there prevails a silent adjective for action; meaningful action. In the business language, an action can translate into a valid profit pertaining to the long-term goal of the organization.

Let me share one of the biggest learning lessons of my life. In my scope of business, most of the meetings take place inside school premises and hard along the aisles of corporate offices. The incident happened a few years ago when I was asked to meet the chairman of a school to discuss my products.

I was given a place to sit as the chairman was preoccupied with some other managerial issues. Fair enough, I took out my mobile phone, sat cross-legged, and kept swiping through my screen. Never could I realize that I was actually oozing arrogance through my demeanor.

It was my version of casually waiting for a prospective client. I was inside the school premise, much within the visible spectrum of the teachers and students. In a few minutes, the chairman's personal assistant came to me and requested me to change my sitting style, for it was unsuitable considering the ambiance. Although I agreed and changed myself, I was never given a chance to meet the chairman. To date, even after accomplishing so many deals, I am not entertained by that particular school.

In due course of time, I realized that it is not only my company's product that will matter in the market but also my own personal profile as the leader. I could have a great team to produce some of the best technology-enabled products; however, how I act to present that product matters the most. A slight hint of arrogance as a leader and your team, stakeholders, and even customers will distance themselves from you.

Right now, I am in that stage of my life where my past glorifies my ability to lead 800 people; however, no one in the present would like to know about my past tenure. Rather, today when/if I am leading just 20 people, the world would like to see how I treat them and produce valuable results for the company.

The same thing applies to the customer-centric market. I can have big honchos as my previous or existing clients; however, none of the next plausible clients will be interested in my relationship with my previous clients. The new clients would take me with their share of perspectives, and every single time, I have to deliver my best in the present.

As my experience says – the past rests in your mind as a lesson learned, while the present comes to you every single day to prove your credibility through actions. Leadership goes through this hamster ring of learning, building credibility, and then taking the most suitable action. The world is watching you, be it in the guise of your customer or the team members.

How unbiased you remain in your actions, how well you lift a demoralized employee, and how you disperse credit to the team efforts, and everything comes under scrutiny before the world bestows you with the crown of a successful leader. As a leader, it is easy to proclaim caring for the team while holding the authority to speak uninterrupted. However, hollowed proclamations die an untimely death. Always; come what may.

Let's understand the concept of hollowed proclamations through this hypothetical case scenario. Mr. X leads a company that deals with women's hygiene products. Due to obvious reasons, a major proportion of the employees are women. Even the company profile proclaims to be fair and unbiased while ticking on the KPIs. There is no gender discrimination per se inside the office ambiance, and everyone works in cohesion with each other.

The marketing department is led by Miss. T, and she has been a great asset to the whole organization. As she witnesses the travel inconvenience faced by many of the employees, she puts a proposal to Mr. X regarding transport facilities for the employees. Considering the core culture of the company, she doesn't discriminate between the male and the female staff. However, during the board meeting, Mr. X cites the financial constraint while also pointing out that the problem is faced only by the female staff. And according to him, the company cannot invest in such one-sided demands.

His statement comes as a shock because a few weeks earlier, Mr. X has spoken in detail about women's safety during the Women's Day celebration. However, most of the employees aren't budged by the non-provision of such an essential facility, and a few eyebrows frown.

A few months pass by, and a pregnant employee is denied maternity leave, citing the work pressure. The management vehemently ignores her past performance record, and eventually, the employee leaves the company. Mr. X's discriminatory actions come under prominence when Miss. T's promotion gets denied based on probable limitations of her gender. The whole organization easily fathoms the inconsistency between X's words and actions.

And gradually, every second employee starts nurturing an element of distrust. The team spirit is lost, productivity declines, and workplace conflicts take center stage.

Does this case sound familiar to you? Leadership is not a façade to create the best impression for the outer world. It is about creating an honest image within and outside the team only to accentuate the overall benefits for every segment of the organization. With the surge of disruptive technology, entrepreneurship has become the new normal while attaching new dimensions to the core concept of leadership. Most millennials do not wish to work under authority and dominance. Rather, they prefer collaboration, authenticity, and team spirit.

According to a survey conducted by Virtuali and Work Place Trends, nearly 50% of the workers believed leadership to be an instrument to empower others. In fact, they don't even mind leaving a job if the leader fails to associate his words with actions.

Leadership spectrum must refract on various elements like – creating a positive team environment, well-informed task delegation, constant engagement and appreciation of employees, and making things more about the team and the organization than about the leader. A leader can hold an encyclopedia of his own achievements and can share all those as personal anecdotes for his team; however, being a good listener is absolutely critical to becoming a good leader. A leader must listen to the people on the front line. Listening enables the leader to learn about the ground realities of the marketplace.

Imagine a situation where the leader has a successful encounter with technology A and tries to influence the team with his past success. One of the team members tries to enlighten him with the new technology B. It is very different from A and is difficult to handle.

Now there can be two situations. In one, the leader sounds boastful and doesn't consider the need for a new or better strategy and keeps demanding better performance from the team without even entering into any action. In the second case, the leader lends an ear to different suggestions and also jumps into action without uttering a single word about past success.

Does that mean a leader's past success never matters? No. It simply means that he has incorporated all the past learnings while chalking out a better proposal for the present team and the problem. And, any day, the second option will be accepted by the team.

For any team to perform well, the work setting should be conducive enough to growth. A leader who leads by action creates a healthy work environment because, at the end of the day, only action produces results. Building relationships, empowering others, and making decisions lead to more effective actions. It is often easier to rephrase your words by coating them with honey, but actions are always transparent. They are visible to the world. You can shout about how well you adjust with your peers and team members and even roam around with a placard of team-worker. But then, what if you always make every argument in the boardroom turn bitter? What if you turn deaf to constructive criticism? This looks like utter hypocrisy when your proclamations fail to translate into action. It is your actions and your team's acceptance, along with the outcomes they produce, that build your reputation as a great leader.

> *"If you make a sale, you can make a living. If you make an investment of time and good service in a customer, you can make a fortune."*
> — Jim Rohn

As I climbed the ladder of success, I realized the significance of the strategic placement of both words and actions. There should always be the right balance of words and actions, be it while getting things done from your team or cracking a deal with your clients. Let's say I am advertising my product to be the best in the market; maybe it is true. I would have taken enough actions to make this world-class product.

However, what if I fail to provide concrete evidence to my clients regarding the efficacy of my product?

My team prepared a great presentation, and the product was also kept on display for the clients to check for its credibility; however, as a leader or the representative of my company, I failed to build an effective storyline regarding my product.

In the world of sales and marketing, storytelling is considered the sharpest tool. A poor storyteller has all the potential to slaughter the greatest of the ideas, while a good narrative can easily make you the center of attraction. Even a daunting concept can be represented with care and compassion if the storyteller is good in his role. As I advocate the right balance between words and action, I do believe that good storytelling has always made a major impact on my team, organization, and also customer base.

No one can deny that the world is full of opposition. Look around, and you will be surprised to find people opposing even essentialities like vaccinations or the right to education. So, does that mean such proposals are inherently wrong? Never. The trick is to build the credibility of yourself and your ideas by letting out a compelling story. That is how a leader can inspire an audience and lead an organization. Effective storytelling is the key when you need to win over a colleague, a team, an executive, a recruiter, or an entire conference audience. Underline the word effectively. Personal anecdotes sow the seed of a boastful attitude in your audience's mind, whereas effective storytelling is the right blend of words and action.

While kindling the right balance between words and action, the leader must be audience-specific. You cannot chalk out the same action for the whole universe.

Becoming audience-specific may sound trivial; however, if you closely analyze the needs of your team and your customers, you will find the significance of becoming audience specific.

Think of it this way. You are authorized to order your subordinate to meet a deadline, but can you order your customer to subscribe to your product within a deadline?

No. As a leader, if you want to know what your target audience is curious about, what worries them, and what motivates them, a series of quick, informal conversations is often the most effective way to figure it out. You can infuse your storytelling to address your audience's specific concerns, while the trick is to avoid bland cliches about your previous successful encounters.

Let me elaborate from the team's perspective. In any organization, the appraisal or promotion is determined through OKR (Objectives and Key Results). Consider a situation when the top management decides to make a universal OKR across all the departments while executing a promotion and appraisal strategy. The HR just puts the notice and vanishes from the scene. The organization has more than 5000 employees, which includes junior and senior executives, new hires, and old employees. They all face the same doubt over having a universal standard. Furthermore, every employee is particularly concerned because this announcement has the potential to impact how all of these different groups will be evaluated and promoted. In that crucial moment, when doubts and anxiety run riot, the employees expect to see the leaders listening to their queries.

As a leader, your role is not restricted to making an audience-specific announcement; rather, you have to contextualize the idea. Many of your team members would have considered the change as yet another random, top-down management initiative. Being their leader, you have to let the whole context explain how it fits into the broader vision of the company, its background, and future strategy. For example, such change in the Edtech industry is quite common. As a leader, I would tread on lines like:

Our previous setup was inherently well-planned, and we all have been executing it well. However, with rapid digitization, we are in dire need of a framework that suits the market demands. As we are widening our prospects and busy enhancing our digital capabilities, we should not escape this new way of setting goals. I am sure, with all of you by my side, we can achieve better productive curves.

Now, the essential requirement is to humanize the words to lighten the mood and illustrate the perspective more effectively. Although artificial intelligence is groping the job market from various angles, we are still working with humans and their emotions. The way leaders speak and the way they carry out themselves behind closed doors are always captured keenly.

There are umpteen cases when a leader has been accused of favoritism for his special inclination toward a particular team member. Such incident demotivates the rest of the employees, and eventually, performance drops. One of the classic examples is promoting the opposite sex. Most workplace conflicts crop up on that premise of favoritism. As a leader, you must be extremely cautious about your public appearance and how you behave. All it needs is a small spark of doubt amongst the team.

On the same note, while striking a balance between anecdotes and action, the leader's storytelling must be followed by action. As often stated, specificity always reduces anxiety. In the same OKR case, if you give your team practical advice and clear direction, you empower them to take action and make your story their own. There can be two narratives to churn out an outcome from the change.

Narrative 1: As a leader, I state the following:

The new system will change the way we work and will redefine success for our company. It will bring us closer to our clients.

Now, all my proclamations are true, and the team agrees to follow the same; however, they hardly understand the sheer significance of setting such goals. Why? Because my statement was just an unhelpful platitude with no concrete proof.

Narrative 2: As a leader, I state the following:

Instead of relying on fixed initiatives and feature launch dates, we will be setting quarterly check-in dates for assessing our progress toward customer metrics like retention, average order value, and customer acquisition cost. In short, executives and middle managers will no longer be prescribing work to product teams. Instead, teams will be responsible for developing their own plans for how best to achieve these goals. Additionally, we will be offering training courses and long-term coaching to support teams as they make this transition. Whenever you are stuck, you are free to reach out to your team leader or even to me. We all are together in this new endeavor.

Now, in this whole hypothetical case scenario, humility is an integral part of the action. While dissecting personal anecdotes, leaders often wince to bare out their failures. But in reality, talking about your failures demonstrates that you're not claiming to have all the answers and that you're willing to learn and adjust course as needed. In my experience, nothing creates a tighter connection between you and your team than acknowledging that you're standing on others' shoulders and you're not going to get everything right all the time. Your surrender shall never let you down but will make you more human in the eyes of your team.

Building a great team needs honest participation and collaboration between the leader and the team members. The crux of leadership lies in the ability to align different groups of people toward a common goal. This, in turn, requires a careful study of individuals and situations, which is why leaders must enter into the virtuous cycle of learning and applying.

Success is never a one-man show. It is a synergy of communication, teamwork, self-development, and the development of others to build productive organizations. Instead of resting on past anecdotes, leaders must be vigilant and must proactively analyze the future, focusing on the hidden opportunities inside the pool of challenges. Leaders must strive to deliver value while building on company strengths and setting the pace to differentiate from the competition.

A leader's most important agenda is to spend time identifying a company's value and having a dynamic debate on how to execute the best plan to bring to market solutions.

Leaders often encounter three critical questions:

- How to turn knowledge into value and decisions?

- Why should you turn decisions into the right actions and behavior?
- How can effectiveness be translated into outstanding results?

If you seek a solution to these questions, none of the answers will highlight past anecdotes. While making an effective decision, a leader must incline toward value. These days, with growing demands, innovation is always in the pipeline, and the leader must be capable of differentiating a generic situation from exceptions. Being a leader, your past experiences can help you assume, but the present situation will need your action to validate that assumption.

On the same note, you can deliver value by converting your decisions into actions. Once your decision is clear and the detailed scope is validated, you as a leader have to follow two steps. At first, you should be looking to gain continuous feedback from the field, both to optimize and nurture adoption and to manage internal bias. Secondly, you must encourage the team to invest in continuous testing against the competitors in the market. In case the customer base is new or the product is not yet visible in the market, as a leader, you have to chalk out a concrete plan to promote your product.

One of the most difficult aspects of business is market education. No matter how much experience you have as a leader, your past anecdotes will eventually become outdated in the changing market. Regular analysis of the market is expensive, laborious, and takes a long time, whether it is done via foot on the ground, digital marketplaces, or online sales and customer services. As a leader, you have to carefully review that the product line and features meet the promise to customers and lay out the benefits and economics. Also, it is you who have to identify and test the messaging to see which one resonates most with customers before asking your team to jump the gun.

Now, while you communicate the organizational value to your team, it is crucial to understand how stakeholders perceive and process information. Each stakeholder holds a specific understanding of contribution, impact, and efficiency. As a leader, you have to strategize your action to fit in the ambiance. Effective leadership builds bridges between knowledge and decisions and between decisions and actions. An effective leader does not roam in the aisle of anecdotes but produces actions as per the situation.

Leaders must understand the need to measure action versus non-action to grow and differentiate a company. Leaders' willingness to act kindle trust. Once a leader is found to be focused on priorities, managing business processes, and educating the market, he enjoys high-level relationship-building skills based on trust, respect, and self-awareness. A leader's job is to cultivate comfortable settings that enhance the confidence of peers to express opinions, brainstorm, and embrace new ideas.

No leader is guaranteed success. A leader must act to produce success. But before you take a dive, as a leader, you must be thoroughly aware of the goal and the desired outcome. Many times, past failures prevent leaders from taking action. However, if you want to escape the world of mediocrity, you have to embrace the power of taking action. As Pablo Picasso said — *Action is the foundational key to all success*. Action shrinks the chances of failure, as whenever you act as a leader, you tend to utilize your existing knowledge to gain more knowledge. Invariably, action leads to a chain reaction. When a team finds the leader taking action, it feels all the more encouraged to work hard.

However, the only cautionary note talks about how far a leader must act. Is it alright for the leader to take every action in his stride? Leaders must be wise enough to know the scope and essentiality of inaction. You must understand that leadership is not about having all the answers. If leaders start providing everything to the team, the chances of innovation become slim.

Being the leader, your employees will always seek a solution from you, and many times your past experience and expertise can tailor-make the solution for them. For a leader, not having a solution is quite an uncomfortable feeling. However, if you always remain the action taker, you can never curate a team with a different skill set. The best leaders empower the team by encouraging creativity. A leader must embrace the notion that sometimes it is better to let the team discover the solution. As you take a backseat and yet participate in a brainstorming session, you strike the right balance between action and delegation.

"While managers try to solve problems, leaders try to create momentum."
— John C. Maxwell

A Quick Fact Check

1. **Do you mean my past experiences should not matter at all?**

Absolutely not. As a leader, your insights and experiences have made you reach this level of expertise. However, the market is continuously evolving. A leader must be vigilant toward his skills and knowledge and must move on with time. Learn from your past but act in the present. Without action, every word remains hollow.

2. **What if I fail to provide a solution being the leader?**

Yes, it is uncomfortable to utter *I don't know*. But unless you say that, you can never turn on your learning mode. A leader's credibility is not belittled by not having an answer but is indeed diminished if he lacks interest in taking action toward finding the answers.

3. **How much action is enough?**

It is a very critical question. An action-oriented leader is always admired; however, that doesn't mean every action should be taken by the leader. Until something is dispersed to the team, the employees will never grow professionally. A leader has to strike the right balance. Let the team handle the challenge first and produce their perspective. Who knows, they may come up with a better solution.

4. **What if I am a new leader and have no anecdotes to share?**

Anecdotes are created by meaningful action. No one is born with success-failure quotes but churn them out while walking on the growth curve. As a newly groomed leader, you will have enough opportunity to create your niche, insights, and experience. The more you learn, and the more you act, the better leader you become to guide your team.

5. Can action make me a Failure-Proof?

There is nothing called fail-proof. However, the more actions you take, the better you are aware of the loopholes, and eventually, you can become Failure-Tolerant.

When Bright Was Not Beautiful!

Here's a story about overconfidence. Every week a new startup proliferates in the Indian market. Bright minds, innovative technologies, never-thought-before ideas, and many such things. However, statistics show that only two out of ten startups can move ahead in time. Half of them fail due to unrealistic goals and mismanagement, and the other half fail due to a lack of funds. Adleaf Technologies fell flat due to both and even more because past anecdotes took prominence instead of necessary actions.

In 2013, Chetan Vashistth jumped into entrepreneurship through Adleaf Technologies. It was a blend of programming bootcamps and software solutions. The business ran well for a while; however, mismanagement through multiple bad business decisions paired with a lack of funds led to the untimely demise of the company. The company started in September when most students start looking for job opportunities if they fail to secure a campus placement. The very first wrong decision was their target audience.

They focused on students appearing for examinations but ignored the recently graduated. The leaders also ignored the sales pipeline and did not take any action to develop newer projects. With a lack of cash flow, conflicts cropped up at the top hierarchy. The leaders failed to construct a business development team even though the technical department was well-equipped. Chetan Vashishtth overlooked the need for a full-time salesperson to sell their boot camp, bring business customers, and supply a trained workforce to consultancy and companies. He was overconfident about his past experiences and presumed that business would come automatically to his company. And this overconfidence killed the future prospects of Adleaf Technologies.

Key Takeaways:

- Align your words and action
- A leader who leads by action creates a healthy work environment
- Leader's actions, team's acceptance, and the outcomes they produce, build the reputation of a great leader
- Never shy away from revealing your failures
- Leaders' willingness to act kindle trust

5

WHAT YOU SEE, GROWS
Possibility or Politics?

> *"It is not possible to have a politics-free organization. The desire for power and control is part of the human nature. Successful business leaders know how to leverage organizational politics by setting performance-oriented instead of resources-oriented political rewards."*
> — Med Jones

Every action a leader takes has a couple of repercussions. The daunting question is how prepared the leader is in case the repercussions brew nasty politics instead of golden opportunities. There are three crucial components of any business organization. People, Process and Politics. Obsessively interlinked, no organization can run without either of them. Also, irrespective of the flawless façade of a company in the market, no business house is immune to organizational politics or conflict because where there are humans, there exists the concept of conflicting opinions and thus grows politics.

However, not all conflicts are injurious to organizational health. Sometimes, conflicting opinions sow the seed of a new perspective of growth.

It all depends on what you as a leader wish to churn out of a conflict — possibility or politics.

Organizations and leadership concepts often revolve around different analogies of ants and snakes. Many of you would have watched documentaries on rattlesnakes on National Geographic Channel. They make a rattling noise before they attack. Most of its prey must quickly recognize the danger to evade it. Toxic leaders carry a close analogy with rattlesnakes. They often carry some particular characteristics and inflict unwanted politics within the organization.

Have you ever come across an *I'm Too Busy* kind of boss? Many leaders often wear the garb of busyness for both defense and offense. They hide from people and their expectations to avoid taking responsibility for finding a solution. Significant levels of disengagement, never being on schedule, never returning calls or replying to emails, talking continuously about being busy, and issuing edicts that make them less approachable are some features that develop ambiguity and mistrust amongst the employees, and in turn, the organization faces negative politics.

Similarly, as a leader, if you take refuge in the blame game and remain the spotlight needy, you create smoke and mirrors in an attempt to make yourself look good and rest as bad. In such cases, even the potential high performer loses interest in the organization. Throwing the team members under the bus, owning team members' accomplishments and being desperate to be noticed, and blaming team members as the cause of every failure brew a terrible scene of organizational politics.

Treading on the same note, ethically challenged leaders tend to build loose relationships and compromise on values. This often kindles the chance of favoritism or sexual prejudices and builds a negative and toxic work culture. In many cases, leaders do performance evaluations as punishment and use the talent development process as a tool to put wrongdoers in their place and punish those who nurture a different opinion.

It is used as a weapon of deflection to cull out team members the leaders don't like. In many toxic work cultures, the leader conducts a performance evaluation in a public forum while making it personal. The moment the leader injects personal bias in evaluating performance, it kindles the doubt of favoritism, and the overall morale of the team goes down.

Consider a leader who shares a personal relationship with one of his team members. Although the team member is not a great performer, he gets a fair share of credit just through that personal inclination. Now, such biases are always visible and remain transparent and eventually let the actual performers doubt the credibility of the leader. In many organizations, leaders nurture a unique mentality that *Loyalty Is Everything*. So, what is wrong with loyalty? After all, loyal employees only can produce results beneficial to the whole organization.

However, in this context, I am talking about promoting personal loyalty toward the leader and not to the organization. Such leaders block transparency in the work culture. Leaders tend to live under the shade while their loyal team members keep away the truth about the happenings. In such cases, the leader maintains a close circle of confidants, and there prevails a fear amongst your team members of uttering the wrong thing. Limited communications with a lot of misdirection and extreme jockeying for positions among team members happen under such circumstances.

Having said that, not all leaders are toxic. Not all leaders work to enjoy personal gains at the cost of the organization and its people. Most successful organizations have leaders who maintain a steady balance between people, processes, and politics. They ensure that people and processes work out at the same pace so that politics do not prey upon either of them. Still, as often found, every action leaves some negative repercussions. After all, you cannot please the whole world with a single idea.

Your proposal or action as a leader may make 80 percent of your staff admire you and follow you. But then, there will always be 20 percent who will sit back and criticize and eventually will light the fire of conflict.

As a leader, you will have two options to face the conflict. Either you can act like a rhinoceros or can become an ostrich. Leaders are human and do experience the fight or flight syndrome when faced with conflict or challenging situations. Your inherent leadership skill decides whether you will approach the conflict like a charging rhinoceros or whether you will stick your head in the sand and avoid them like an ostrich.

In case you believe in the latter, just understand that problems never disappear magically. Any organization grows due to a chain reaction. Every single employee act as a catalyst to transform the process into a product. Leaders of healthy, positive work cultures ensure the foundation of the value is solid and woven throughout the organization. Leaders' role is to ensure the talent review, people development, rewards, and recognition are fair and focused on actual performance, not likability or popularity. As a leader, it is essential to cultivate transparent, direct communications throughout the organization and all teams.

In pursuit of doing and directing, leaders' action becomes visible to the whole organization. As a leader, you would have chalked out a plan of acting and delegating after foreseeing a fruitful possibility; however, people around you may not understand your stand and may churn out politics.

Let's understand this concept with a hypothetical case scenario. You are leading a team of twenty members, and you have a deadline to meet while producing your product for a very important client. You choose X to do the job on a priority basis, although the whole team knows that Y is the best man to do that kind of job. Apparently, X is your college junior, and you already share a good rapport with him. And, there were a few past incidents where you had praised Y's work ethic but pointed out his comparatively slower pace.

You have two deadlines back-to-back, and you choose X over Y for making the preliminary arrangements without giving any justification for your action.

In a week's time, a rumor makes its way to the office that X is your blue-eyed boy and you are giving all significant projects to him. Many employees start showing their displeasure toward X and you. The situation turns bitter as the team members start distancing themselves from X, and he gets no assistance from anyone. No one in the team confronts you or asks for a justification, and X keeps suffering for your opaque decision-making process. With no cooperation from the team, X's productivity loses the sheen, and the team fails to make an impact on the client.

On the forefront, X's potential gets misjudged without realizing the crux of the matter. Now, who is the ultimate loser in this case? X or the leader? I would say the organization has lost a good opportunity with a client because you, as a leader, have failed to maintain transparency in your action.

Visualize the same scenario from another perspective. I am the leader, and I choose X over Y to do this particular task. While assigning the task to X, I decided to discuss the whole deadline issue openly with both X and Y. I delegated the work to X but under the supervision of Y as the latter is more experienced. I create a win-win situation for both the employees and also for the organization as talent is restored and the deadline is also met.

The core idea is to see the hidden possibility in every challenge. The more you look for the possibility, the less you ignite politics. A leader's role is to extract the possibilities for the greater good. As the number of people grows in an organization, the process must be suitably streamlined, where every individual is given the due importance to play their specific role. As every individual's job description is streamlined solely based on merit, people and process maintain a steady pace toward growth.

When leaders make their thinking visible, the chance of organizational politics is dramatically reduced. As a leader, if I nominate a particular person for a specific task, I must make known to the whole team the reason behind my decision. I must cite the person's credibility based on his past performance, but at the same time, I should also encourage the other members to come forward with their opinion if they think they can do it better.

Now, in most cases, hardly anyone wishes to cross-examine a leader's decision. Sometimes out of respect or fear, while at times avoiding responsibility. An added project is, of course, an added baggage in the routine job. But then, here comes the leader's role in checking for all the probable options. Until I encourage a newer perspective in the field, I block the scope of innovation. Also, the more I remain inclined to the existing talent based on their past exposure and performance, I tend to build a nest of favoritism. My team may not be vocal about that, but whispers shall definitely make the rounds.

Good leadership stems from strong organizational culture. Harold S. Geneen, the once president and CEO of International Telephone and Telegraph Corp. (ITT), is famous for growing the company from a medium-sized business with $765 million in sales in 1961 into an international conglomerate with $17 billion in sales in 1970. He extended its interests from the manufacturing of telegraph equipment into insurance, hotels, real estate management, and other areas and transformed ITT into the archetypal modern multinational conglomerate. He had wonderful insight into the idea of building a productive and positive organization.

In his own words — *Every company has two organizational structures: The formal one is written on the chart; the other is the everyday relationship of the men and women in the organization.*

Never believe that uncooked truth that every corner is a plethora of possibilities. Politics and possibilities are sown through actions. As a leader, you can churn on better possibilities once you sew alignment in the company's objectives and its employees' motivations. By building continuous alignment to their vision, purpose, and goals, leaders can avoid politics. Secondly, the moment leaders nurture a culture of appreciation and frequent recognition of every performer without having any biases, and employees get a sense of ethical leadership. Trust is vital to an organization. When a leader's thinking is visible to the team and action is transparent, the team understands the bigger goal and always works in collaboration to produce better results.

Great companies preach a culture that means business. Talented employees motivate each other to excel, while the leaders help to bridge the skill gap by upskilling the mediocre performers. A great leader encourages teamwork that encompasses collaboration, communication, and respect between team members. When everyone on the team supports one another, employees will get more done and feel happier while doing it. Business organizations are not a one-man army. Integrity forms the core and is vital to all teams when they rely on each other to make decisions, interpret results, and form partnerships.

On the same note, honesty and transparency are critical components to avoid any undue conflict. Similarly, a leader who is constantly looking for possibilities must have innovation by his side. A culture of innovation means that you apply creative thinking to all aspects of your business, even if that means you have to overlook the seniority of a team member.

Much like how culture is an integral part of an organization's growth, the conflict remains the major deterrent. Missing a deadline and conflict slowly distills between employees and the immediate boss. Being younger, if you lash out at a senior colleague, you are bound to get hate-zoned. And then, as a leader, if you disagree with a supplier or a client, you are sometimes digging your own grave. Conflict is multidimensional and can attack you from any corner. On a closer analysis, there are three sources of politics or conflict. It can be task conflict, relationship conflict, or value conflict.

Task conflict involves concrete issues related to employees' work assignments and can consist of disputes regarding how to divide resources, differences of opinion on procedures and policies, managing expectations at work, and judgments and interpretation of facts. Assume a scenario where you are a young, dynamic leader and have joined the organization to inject the new wave of innovative work style.

You have two very senior members working under you who refuse to change their conservative style. Although you cite enough reasons to justify your style of conduct, they prepare a robust opposition and, in turn, create a toxic mindset against you.

As you are the new leader, many of the team members fall prey to their version of the story. Now, how can you deal with the situation? Should you raise the problem to your higher-ups? Never. Escalation of problems hardly helps; firstly, because communication is diluted, and secondly, you will make a mockery of yourself both before your team and your higher-ups. In such situations, you can focus on identifying the deeper interests underlying parties' positions. Participate in active listening and ask deeper questions to the whole team without judging the conflict creators.

There should always be a WHY behind their reluctance, so listen to it out. On the other hand, engage the parties in a collaborative problem-solving process in which they brainstorm the possible solutions to the issues. When parties reach to solution by working together, instead of an outcome imposed upon them, they are more likely to be sticking to the agreement and get along better in the future.

The second major source of politics is relationship conflict. An organization is built with different kinds of people who come from different backgrounds clinging to their own lifestyle, mindset, and social upbringing. It's not that all of us are raised to believe in altered sexual orientation; however, that kind of belief should be restricted to our personal domain. The organization needs better performers, which is nowhere connected to a leader's personal opinion of the LGBTQ community.

Consider you are running an advertising agency and have your own reservations toward gay marriage. Your graphic designer is a master at his work and asks for an appraisal. Should you consider his work or his sexual preferences? The moment you deny the appraisal without citing any flaw in his performance, you open the door of doubt.

Quite on the same thread falls the third source of politics – value conflict. It comprises political, religious, ethical, normative, and other firmly held ideas. Although discussion of politics and religion in the workplace is frequently frowned upon, disagreements regarding values can occur in the context of work and policies.

Let's assume the leader asks a Muslim employee to work on Eid just because the company doesn't declare a holiday on Muslim festivities. Disputes involving values tend to heighten defensiveness, distrust, and alienation. In value-based conflict, it is better to have a cognitive understanding in which the leader and the team member reach an accurate conceptualization of one another's point of view. It doesn't require sympathy or emotional connection, only a "values-neutral" ability to describe accurately what someone else believes about the situation.

Having said that, possibilities and politics are not restricted only to the team you lead. When there are so many stakeholders in a business, politics can thrive in every possible way. Consider the same value-based conflict rising with a supplier. Just because your views vary, you, as a leader, cannot force a supplier to work on something that undermines his core belief.

The organizational conflict has both positive as well as negative connotations and consequences. As a leader, the conflict must be managed for organizational benefit. There are umpteen business articles that speak about managers spending nearly twenty percent of their time dealing with conflict situations. The more the business grows, the greater number of stakeholders get attached to the business. The increased number of human interactions eventually led to different kinds of politics at both individual, interpersonal and intergroup levels.

Consider a situation where the boss asks his secretary to prevent a vendor from meeting him. Lying is something very unethical, according to the secretary, and she starts doubting the ethics of her boss. The vendor keeps visiting every alternate day and somehow releases his frustration on the secretary.

One fine day, the secretary spills the bean, and the vendor forces himself to meet the boss. The situation turns grim as the boss loses his trust in the secretary, and the vendor also decides to get out of the deal due to the boss's unethical behavior. A small lie becomes huge chaos, and ultimately the organization suffers a significant amount of loss.

It is a classic example of organizational politics stemming out of an individual's personal value system. This kind of politics works out when a person has to choose between two equally desirable alternatives or between two equally undesirable goals. In this case, the boss never gave a valid justification while asking the secretary to lie. Instead of making the vendor come to him every alternate day, the boss could have had an open talk with the vendor, citing some valid reasons.

On the other hand, interpersonal conflict happens amid competition. For example, two employees who are competing for limited capital and resources often churn out nasty politics. This situation can become further acute when scarce resources cannot be shared and must be obtained. Let's say there are two equally deserving professors, both up for promotion. However, only one of them can be bestowed with the position because of budget and positional constraints. This can lead to interpersonal conflict between the two professors. Moreover, the professor who fails to get the promotion nurture the idea of favoritism against the management. In a similar scenario, let's assume two marketing managers are arguing over promotional methods to induce higher sales. Conflicts happen when they put their personal opinions before facts. Opinions that are provided are highly personal and subjective and may provide for disagreements and criticism.

Now, it is the leader's duty to find out the source of such conflict that is creating negative politics in the organization. An organization can be stated as an interlocking network of groups, departments, sections, or work teams. If we look at intergroup conflicts, it is not so much personal but due to factors inherent in the organizational structure.

One of the most typical disagreements is between the organization's line managers and its employees. Line managers may be resentful of their reliance on workers for information and suggestions. The personnel may be resentful of their inability to immediately execute their own ideas and recommendations. Intergroup conflict results from this dependency.

Inter-unit disputes can also arise as a result of uneven incentives and varying performance requirements for various units and groups. For example, salespeople who rely on commission as a form of compensation for their efforts may promise their clients a particular quantity of the product and delivery timeframes that the manufacturing department may find hard to satisfy, resulting in friction between the two departments.

Similarly, different functional groups within the organization may come into conflict with each other because of their different specific objectives. In any organization, small or big, there are some fundamental differences in the structure, operations, and processes among different units, and thus each unit develops its own organizational sub-structure.

These sub-structures differ in goal orientation which can be highly specific for production but highly fluid for research and development. Time orientation also differs, like the short run for sales and the long run for research. Also, supervisory styles differ; one region may be more democratic than another.

Sales and production are two basic examples of inter-unit friction. The sales department is often customer-oriented and desires to have high stocks in order to satisfy orders as they come in. It is a pricey choice as compared to the manufacturing department, which is concerned with cost-effectiveness and keeping as few finished goods on hand as possible. Intergroup conflict may also emerge between day and night shift workers, who may blame each other for anything that goes wrong, from misplaced tools to maintenance issues.

Let me share a slice from my personal experience. When we started as a startup, it was just a team of 5 members. Gradually it grew to 20, then 150, and right now, we are 2000+ people in the organization. In this course of growth, as a leader, I found the biggest loophole was dug when the process was not clear to the staff.

In due course of time, I found teams working in silos. There was a dearth of cohesion between the marketing team and the customer service department.

The marketing team was never available on weekends, while the customer service section was always working to address the customers' concerns. Eventually, two teams came to loggerheads. The employees who had to go on field trips had no particular time schedule for their job, while the marketing team was enjoying a 9-5 schedule. There prevailed a communication gap as the timing never matched. As we kept growing, we had to find a solution to streamline the whole process so that the human resource and operations work in cohesion with each other.

The organization grew faster, and we had to jot down the job specificities for every employee. Ten people doing ten different jobs without maintaining any balance and collaboration could never be fruitful for the organization. Whether it was financial management or an operational hiccup, every department had to be in collaboration with the customer management section. If the finance section failed to meet the deadline, the customer service department had to face the brunt for no mistake of its own. This kind of situation cropped up even with the other partners in supply chain management.

For example, if the payment was delayed from the finance section, the operational unit faced the brunt as the supplier declined to supply. In due course of time, as a leader, I had to mend the bridge between the different departments by letting them know the final organizational goal. Working in silos could never make us what we are today. Now, there were situations when the conflict was more inter-organizational.

The problem showed its face in the supply chain unit. As a leader, it would have been easy for me to raise the issue with the national head; however, very soon in my career, I realized that problems do not get solved vertically. The solution must be worked out horizontally as escalation causes more rift.

If the problem is happening at the regional level, it has to be worked out at the same level. Your national head might use his influence against the troublemaker in the supply chain; however, he may not be available all the time. At the same time, the supply chain worker will have a bigger influence at the ground level.

As I climbed the ladder, I realized that every negative political scenario stems from some of the key factors. Lack of clarity regarding the person who is responsible for which section of a task or project produces a negative impact on the overall performance. As a leader, the moment you define the roles and responsibilities of the team members, they all will know how to approach the situation. Similarly, favoritism, even if disguised, causes a rift. Consider a situation where as a leader, you tend to do too much for one particular employee just because he is a mediocre performer. Once or twice, it is acceptable, but not every time. The market is full of talent, and the other members of the team would see your action as practicing partiality.

Improper resource allocation kindles the idea of favoritism if you, as a leader, do not make your stand clear to the whole organization. And lastly, when there is disorientation between the personal goals of the individual and the goals of the organization, a conflict of interest arises. As a leader, it is really important for you to be vigilant that you are choosing the right member for your organization.

Change is the biggest contributor to organizational politics. Whether it is hierarchical restructuring or change in the system of operation and appraisal, conflict is bound to happen. In such cases, leaders must not work in a reactionary mode; rather, they should drive politics in a very productive manner by taking up proactive measures that diminish any negativity.

One way to minimize the power of politics is by redirecting the activity. A good leader should shift the focus to the qualities and requirements of the company by ensuring a transparent work culture where every employee is held accountable for their actions. Even the leader.

Let's say the previous requirements are altered, and then the leader should educate the staff about what is currently needed for promotion or navigating the change. You have to turn the attention to standards by openly discussing what the new standard will be and the qualifications needed to take part in the new system.

A leader must keep politics to a dull roar by clearly communicating how the company is doing. For example, if the integration of a new software system is not working out, you have to be open about the delay. In case of unexpected roadblocks, talk to the employees while giving details about the final goal and the plan for overcoming the obstacles. A good system of communication will help you to find out more possibilities amid politics.

What you see as a leader will grow in the organization. Internal politicking, when used effectively, can assist in finding compromises to tricky workplace situations and problems. It often helps in executing a strategy and remains a valuable tool to effect organizational change. Office politics is an unavoidable element of the job, but it is not necessarily a detrimental force. If not addressed, it may lead to a hostile workplace, low team morale, and lower productivity. However, it may also have a beneficial impact on achieving organizational goals, particularly when managing change projects. To mitigate the negative consequences, leaders must maintain their finger on the pulse, be open and honest, and encourage collaborative working.

> *"There are three ways of dealing with difference: domination, compromise, and integration. By domination, only one side gets what it wants; by compromise, neither side gets what it wants; by integration, we find a way by which both sides may get what they wish."*
> — Mary Parker Follett

As the saying goes, the pinnacle is quite lonely; however, the view is quite wonderful. A leader, sitting on the top, can get a grasp of who is what in a team. There will be The Complainers, who are always unhappy sucking away the positivity from the organization. Then, there are The Gossipers who would love to create stories that would pierce the whole work culture with a sharp blade of intentional untruth. As a leader, you will also encounter Sandbaggers who thrive on sandbagging those who they feel threatened by through their passive-aggressive behavior.

On the other hand, The Confronters will use their mental and physical brute to overpower the meek. And, amidst this pandemonium of human conflict and office politics, possibilities linger around the real performers. The silent ones who are clear with their personal and organizational goals and make their work do the talking.

As a leader, it is your responsibility to check who is exhibiting what and what you can extract from an employee's hidden potential. Efficient leadership runs on the parallel track of exhibiting and extracting talent.

A Quick Fact Check

1. **Oh! I love this Cold War between my two managers. Their competitive mindset is helping the company's overall performance.**

No. Never. Unhealthy competition is never good for any organization. In their chase to impress you, they are inflicting negative politics in the whole workplace. In times of crisis, you will see a dearth of collaboration between the teams, and eventually, the company will be at a loss.

2. **If I choose a person based on performance, then why am I called an advocate of favoritism?**

Is your action visible to the whole organization? Do you justify your course of action? If you keep on assigning the high-priority task to one particular individual without extracting the potential of others, you are advocating favoritism.

3. **Politics is bad. Should I avoid it?**

The Ostrich effect is more prominent when it comes to office politics. As an employee, you can have the option of avoiding office politics but never as a leader. Your avoidance will be mirrored as your approval of negative work culture. As a leader, you should seek a solution and not sit back and enjoy the melodrama.

Not Everything Is That Bad

All office politicking is not necessarily evil. According to Gerald Ferris, a Professor at the University of Florida and co-author of the book Political Skill at Work: Truly skillful execution of the behaviors associated with politics is usually perceived as genuine, authentic, straightforward and effective." The winning line is if you play office politics well, you won't be called political, and rather you will be called good with people.

Key Takeaways:
- People, Process, and Politics are three irreplaceable components of any business organization
- Leaders must maintain a steady balance between people, processes, and politics
- Organizational politics cannot be avoided, but leaders must check for the hidden possibilities
- Make your thinking visible to reduce the chances of politics
- Leaders must dig deeper into the real reason behind the ongoing politics
- A good system of communication help leaders to find out more possibilities amid politics

6

EXTRACT AND EXHIBIT

Quality either voices out or walks out!!!

Ajay is a technical content writer in one of the top consultancy services in the country. Quiet and composed, he prefers to mind his business at work. It is not like he does not befriend a colleague or remains a recluse, but it is more like his inherent nature not to exhibit too much of his accomplishments. He prefers to remain silent and lets his work do the talking. Vincent is the team lead for the technical content writing team. Thriving in the opposite spectrum, he is jovial, talkative, quite boastful, and of course, a proficient extractor of work. In short, Vincent knows the quick tricks to get on the top. Every member of the team is very well aware of his sleight of hand; some leave no stone unturned to impress him and roam in the aisle of YES BOSS. At the same time, there are a few, like Ajay, who feel that their performance should be appreciated more than their personal inclination toward the immediate boss.

During the last appraisal meeting, the top management credited Vincent for a project that was solely accomplished by Ajay. Not even once Ajay's name was mentioned.

Neither the top leader enquired about the team behind the success nor did Vincent utter a word. He took every ounce of appreciation on his shoulder and, in fact, boasted it before Ajay and others. A couple of months pass by, and eventually, every successful endeavor of Ajay ends up getting credit to Vincent and no one else. On the other hand, Vincent shamelessly keeps delegating tasks without even bothering to share a note of gratitude. The top leader sees Vincent as a credible performer and promotes him in every corporate event, while Ajay keeps slogging to pave the path of prosperity for Vincent.

One fine day, Ajay decides to leave this job and submits his resignation letter. As the top management is completely unaware of his potential, they don't budge. His resignation is approved. Now, hell breaks on Vincent's head. He knows that he can never maintain his success quotient without a top performer like Ajay. Vincent goes out of their way to persuade Ajay to remain in the company. Ajay, on the other hand, has already got a better opportunity in a rival company, and he has been very open about the toxic and ignorant work culture of his present company.

Vincent knows his managerial flaws but cannot tell the top management. During the notice period, the top leader receives the complete story and understands the grave mistake he has committed by shirking away from his own role. He should have been way more vigilant in his approach while checking the KPIs. To crosscheck the authenticity of the situation, the top leader gives one exclusive work to Vincent. The final outcome, though, is good but is not up to the previous standard. The top leader could easily make out a difference and holds a one-to-one meeting with Ajay.

The complete picture stands bare in front of the top management, and they could sense the kind of reputation they are building in the market if people like Ajay keeps leaving the company. Apparently, a few from other teams also walk on the same path and cite the kind of work culture that has been nurtured by the skip-level managers. Soon, the persuasion process starts. Initially, only through motivational words and then slowly migrates to giving a better salary.

Eventually, the top management fathoms the bigger loss they are facing because of their ignorance toward the parallel track of management. They have been nurturing the process of extraction of work while forgetting that it is equally important to keep a close watch on who is exhibiting what and how much authenticity lies in that exhibition.

In the above case scenario, when the top management sat to persuade Ajay, it seemed like an eyewash. As a high-performing employee, Ajay had expected the top leader's intervention a long time ago. Every employee holds their unique potential; however, only some are good to exhibit in public. People like Ajay are silent killers. They kill critics for their performance, and at the same time, when/if they are not appreciated appropriately, they have the power to massacre the company's overall performance and reputation by leaving the job. It is, of course, true that the market is flooded with talent. If one Ajay goes, a hundred Ajays will come in. However, rapid attrition is never good for any organization. It creates a bad rapport and has a detrimental effect on the productivity of the whole organization.

Treading on the same note, extraction and exhibition must work out parallelly. A leader's prime role is to construct a high-performing team. Inherently, humans are lazy and always seeking comfort. It indeed feels good to earn a handsome salary without doing much work. However, with the right kind of people and the right kind of leader, every individual is motivated to move closer to the organizational goal.

A leader must identify the right kind of people in the talent pool. Not every performer is verbose; similarly, not every talkative employee is unproductive. Performance potential should be evaluated thoroughly and diligently to understand the authenticity of a performer. While extracting work from the employees, leaders must understand that mere motivation may not work. Ownership of tasks and skillful education are two powerful ways to get subordinates working to their full potential.

Great leaders often use motivation as their weapon to get things done because a more productive team helps in meeting elusive sales goals, raising workplace morale, and revitalizing the company. But sometimes, employees are unwilling to comply, and as a leader, you may have to follow up with a tougher course of action.

There is always a need to set the tone in the workplace by incorporating a *can-do* attitude. A leader has to become the encourager-in-chief in the workplace. While trying to extract work, mere delegation will never work; after all, it is human resources and not machine resources. Humans work with their emotions attached. A leader has to show confidence in the employee's ability. Let's assume you have hired a salesman who is good at communicating in Hindi but falters in English. His salesman skill is par excellence, but he is losing out on confidence because his peers are quite extravagant in showing off their English skills.

Now, as a leader, you have to be vigilant toward this mushrooming conflict. The organization needs a good salesman at the moment and not an English scholar. Language skill is needed according to the target market. If your company is selling a product in the northern belt of India, there is no harm in taking a salesman proficient in Hindi. Why would you need an English speaker? As a leader, it invariably becomes your task to see that the hired salesman is not cocooning inside self-deprecation. You have to nurture true talent and extract work from them. Now, while nurturing talent, you must cross-examine if you are nurturing the right candidate or not. In Ajay-Vincent's case, the top leader kept nurturing Vincent when he was never the right candidate.

But then, how to find who the right person is? Come out of the cabin and get dirty in the field. Delegation, direction, and action walk on one track, and vigilance walk on a parallel track. A leader has to be a keen observer of people. When you are chairing an appraisal meeting, you must be capable of seeing through the performer. Scrutinize every performance and look for the silent killers in the team. The world is full of people who still believe that their work will speak for them.

At the same time, there are scavengers in every workplace who are potent stealers of others' credit. Therefore, as you try to churn out possibilities amid all the politics of the workplace, you should be capable of verifying the authenticity of the exhibition.

While extracting work, the company's vision should be crystal clear for every member of the team. Employees must work toward the organizational benefit and not for the leader's benefit. Let me make you revisit the coffee story. When you are hired, you are hired for the organization and not to please a particular boss. As an employee, your role is described in your job profile; however, you invariably become more inclined to build a better relationship with your immediate supervisor. Eventually, in your pursuit to impress the boss, you forget that you are not there in the organization to serve coffee and cookies to your boss. You are there to meet the organizational goal.

Let's say Mr. D is hired as a coder. His job profile is to develop codes according to the client's demands. There is a standardized procedure to be followed from client acquisition to the final delivery of the product. D's immediate boss gets a friend on board as a client and asks D to make amendments in the regular course of action. Now, D is in a dilemma. His performance appraisal form is going to be filled out by this immediate boss. If he disagrees, he may not get the promotion and thus breaks the rule. D's flexibility is noticed by his immediate boss, and gradually he starts building and bending the rules for his personal benefit. D keeps slogging at the cost of the company's resources but for the personal benefit of the boss. In due course of time, the top management discovers the loophole and throws out D for meddling with the rules.

Now, let me ask you if it was entirely D's fault. It is a preconceived notion to please the immediate boss to avail of promotions. In this pursuit, every employee forgets the larger goal in the picture. As a top leader, if you start having personal interaction with every employee (occasionally), you can get a clearer picture of the whole process. There is a high probability of skip-level managers running their parallel governance.

An employee's true potential can be unleashed when they are allowed to participate in decision-making. Involve subordinates in some of the decision-making processes and grant them authority to make decisions according to their ability and proven track record. For example, just because you get a new recruit with better qualifications, you cannot abandon the experience of an older employee who knows the organization far better than the new recruit.

Instead of training the new recruit under you, the older employee can always be given a chance to train the newbies. Similarly, when you include employees while making some critical decisions, you provide them with a sense of ownership. Remember, a man who owns something will always preserve that something.

There is another wonderful way to extract talent. A team always has three categories of the performer; top, mediocre and slow. The top performers can be paired with the less productive people and can mentor them well to reach the goal. But here, the cautionary note is; everyone should be a contributor to the overall effort. Let's say Ajay is the top performer on the team, and he is a workaholic. Purab is a poor performer and also a big-time shirker. He fathoms Ajay's weakness and starts exploiting it by citing his personal incapacities. One day he shies away, stating his ill health. The other day he introduced family problems, and the process goes on. Ajay, on the other hand, wants to get the job done, and he completes the task on his own. The team leader gets the impression that Ajay would have taught Purab how to do the task. However, the reality is different. In due course of time, the management assumes that the whole team is performing while, in reality, it is only Ajay whose talent and skill are extracted but hardly exhibited.

In such disguised situations, leaders should meet the employees personally to check the whole course of their performance. There is no harm in telling the employee that they have been observed. It is not about threatening them but ensuring that they know they are retained by the organization on the basis of their performance and not what colorful façade they exhibit.

In Ajay-Purab's case, the leader must keep a close eye on both of them. Ajay's workaholism can impart better results for the whole organization; however, if Purab never learns the job, the organization will suffer as and when Ajay leaves. Moreover, what is the use of investing resources in people like Purab? Employees like Purab are omnipresent and hold an attitude problem. Their outlook is unhealthy for the overall growth of an organization.

In an organizational setup, umpteen comments run in the corridors and are always riddled with subjectivity. Do we not hear comments like *That employee has an attitude problem, He is a shirker,* or *She is the gossipmonger.* These are indeed negative comments or negative attitudes that brew more politics than a possibility. As a leader, before you can take effective action to guide or correct an employee's attitude in your business, you must clearly define what is negative. Once you are clear about what constitutes negativity in your workplace, you can take the necessary steps to address your employee's problem and stop the spread of negativity that can infect your workplace.

The first step is to create and sustain team connections. When a leader engages in supportive conversations with staff without resorting to complaining and belittling comments, it promotes a collaborative environment. Negativity is often a performance issue. If you have a closer look, people, performance, and politics are closely associated with each other. And performance and politics are inversely proportional.

The more the politics grow, the less the performance will be. A leader must address an employee's inability to work in a team situation and also speak to a worker's dismissive behavior. There should always be a WHY behind an action and also inaction. However, while confronting an issue, it is always better to have evidence. As a leader, you have to specify instances of negative attitude you have observed or about which other workers have complained. Also, it is your job to provide a supportive environment to address their problems.

Many times, top performers become so boastful of their accomplishments that they start belittling others. As a leader, it is also important for you to understand that organizations run on team efforts. Every employee carries their unique talent and skill, and that should be presented on the table. Just because a person is better looking or better at talking, it doesn't mean that he is the ultimate asset for the company. A leader must be able to differentiate between confidence and arrogance and should have an eye for building and retaining the right kind of team.

Whether it is a startup or an international behemoth, success lies in a great team. A team is essential to allow any endeavor to grow scale that would be literally impossible for only one person to do. A successful team starts with the hiring of the right people who are working toward the common goal, are the kind of people who are goal-oriented, and respect the hierarchical structure of the organization. Even the most innovative entrepreneurs cannot transform an idea into success without having a proper team. No matter how good the business idea is, it cannot be a proper business without a dynamic team working cohesively to execute a shared business plan.

Let's take the example of our national cricket team. Sachin Tendulkar has been the biggest asset of our Indian Cricket. But could India win a match without having the rest of the ten players? A business is no different. The business team you assemble as a leader should contain complementary skill sets such that the team can accomplish tasks that you, as the team leader, could not do on your own. You need a team since every firm has its own corporate structure, company culture, and unique set of workers who each offer years of expertise. Getting the appropriate group of individuals does not happen by chance. It takes careful nurturing from a team leader who understands the team's beliefs, goals, and code of ethics. Without this top-down leadership, your employees are merely coworkers. It is up to the leader to build an effective team by extracting the right potential and appreciating the right people.

Let me share some insight on how to do that.

Establish expectations from day one

Although cliched, the phrase *nature abhors a vacuum* is true. New employees and new team members somehow arrive as relatively blank slates while being open to an array of company cultures. However, to survive in this competitive market, they quickly start seeking cues for how to operate as a member of your company. A leader must seize this opportunity. Establish ground rules and make your expectations clear from the start—not only in terms of sales targets or a five-year strategy but also in terms of the sort of team atmosphere you foster. If you want to foster a culture of shared accountability, problem-solving, and decision-making, you must communicate these principles from the beginning and on your own. Skip-level managers should not intervene and start a parallel organization.

Nurture respect for talent

At work, you want your employees to be part of a team, but you also need to keep in mind that these are people with their own experiences. Your own prejudices should not be considered when evaluating their talent. Every employee has gotten thus far in life without your guidance, and they likely have full and varied lives outside of work. Humans are not robots; they need recognition. Individuals who are appreciated and valued for their particular abilities and ability to contribute to your shared objective create a strong team atmosphere.

Engender connections within the team

Being the leader, you value and honor each individual member of the team, but how far the team members are exhibiting that same respect and care toward one another.

Practice emotional intelligence

Emotional intelligence is important to great leaders. Members of the team are not live drones. Every person has a unique set of requirements. Some team players thrive on pursuing common objectives. Others prefer healthy rivalry, whether with an outside opponent or another sales team inside the same workplace. By accepting the realities of varied work styles and motivational techniques, you must treat people's individual characteristics as an advantage, not an impediment.

Choose appreciation over criticism

Honey attracts more flies than vinegar. When it comes to attracting talent, positive reinforcement is more successful than negative reinforcement. You must resist the desire to point out flaws. Instead, support the team and build a pleasant team atmosphere by mentioning events and actions that you really enjoyed. Positive reinforcement is significantly more effective than condemning individuals who fail to create outcomes in driving team performance.

Use the power of effective communication

We all want to know where we stand as humans. Are my coworkers satisfied with the work I'm doing? Is there anything I need to work on? When your subordinates perceive that you are upset but do not express it, they become worried and perform poorly. In another example, if they believe they are doing a wonderful job but you as a manager aren't pleased, they may be taken aback when you inform them that they have been underperforming. As a leader, you must practice your communication abilities; great communication may sustain professional relationships for decades, whereas silence can swiftly destroy them.

Always reward good work

People love affirmation of their hard work. If you're fortunate enough to be able to give financial bonuses, well and good; however, there are many ways to thank the performers. An easy way is to practice the art of delegating. If a team member shows great judgment, allow them to make some key decisions that you may have once reserved for yourself. If they are particularly responsible with money, give them authority to make some financial decisions. There are many small ways to show that you're paying close attention to your employees and that their efforts are appreciated. It will reflect well on you as a leader and help remind people that they are valued members of the team.

Diversify

Diverse talent is necessary for growth. People with different backgrounds, experiences, ages, and opinions bring better perspectives to the table. As a leader, you have to hire and retain people with the goal of covering your blind spots. Always surround yourself with people who will inform the judgment calls you make and the content you put out.

Build a trustworthy team

A high-performing team needs self-starters. Someone who can make decisions on your behalf and who's going to be a good ambassador for the organization is your first go-to person in times of growth as well as crisis. Always remember, a king needs effective ministers. Groom them to be collaborators by empowering them to make leadership decisions on their own. You're investing time and resources into this person, so consider their potential for longevity at your company or within your industry.

> *"Building a cohesive leadership team is the first critical step that an organization must take if it is to have the best chance at success."*
> — Patrick Lencioni

In the scope of positive psychology, leadership is often tagged with the term personal effectiveness. It advocates individuals' personal utilization of all skills, talent, and energy to achieve goals. Personal effectiveness integrates a lot of features:

- Provide high-quality work
- Make people happy

- Create and keep successful relationships
- Positively influence people
- Advances in career
- Earn respect from colleagues
- Become an expert in a specific dimension

On the global platform of flourishing business, we can find these features present in all the successful leaders who could build and retain high-performers in their organization and lead the organization toward greater success. The present CEO of Google and its mother company Alphabet, Sundar Pichai, is considered one of the greatest leaders of the present time. His good communication skills, effective decision-making, and critical thinking have made the world witness the making of a true leader. It is not his knowledge of products and technology but his skill in working with people that could make him stand out. One of his greatest skills is leading people to greater heights of their skills. Pichai is an inclusive leader or, rather, a team player who believes in empowering people. His resilience toward any difficulty makes him a true leader, and the big success of Google Chrome is proof of his resilience.

Pichai is a firm believer in *People Come First*. He encourages cooperation and collaboration. In his leadership, the true potential of an individual comes out, and Google has become one of the topmost market leaders in this present scenario.

In one of his interviews, Pichai opined that sometimes he had to make hard decisions in a critical situation. And as he was confident enough on his team, he could take the critical steps. In his own words — Someone who can make choices on your behalf and who will be a good spokesperson for the organization is your first point of contact during times of development and crisis. Remember that a monarch needs efficient ministers. Prepare them to be collaborators by giving them the authority to make leadership decisions on their own. You're spending time and money on this person, so think about their long-term potential at your firm or in your sector. Pichai's sheer adulation for innovative ideas has encouraged the younger breeds of Google to diversify better. Making the correct and exact decision in favor of the organization's growth is one of his fortes.

In the present times, he is amongst the most-loved CEOs. As an active leader, a positive personality and self-confidence are essential factors in nurturing a better team. A leader must manage all kinds of threats and issues cropping up in the organization and manage proper work structure by pushing the right talent. A leader holds the responsibility to manage organizational activities and employee retention issues. Apart from the external growth of an organization, the leader must maintain harmony inside the organization.

Simple ignorance of the right talent is detrimental to human capital management. Human resource is the biggest asset of any organization. A leader must understand employee retention risks and implement strategies to reduce talent attrition rates. The cost of employee turnover is incredibly high. It impacts operational costs, revenue, productivity, company culture, customer experience, and almost every facet of organizational goals.

If you dig deeper into a comprehensive human capital management strategy, you will find a robust plan for retaining valuable employees, which your organization took time to recruit, onboard, and train. Statistically, the cost to replace an employee can range from one-half to two times the employee's annual salary. Leaders who fail to prioritize employee retention clearly pay a steep price.

However, those who invest in improving employee retention and addressing turnover risks earn significant rewards. Talent retention has its own perks toward sales growth, improved productivity and work quality, as well as higher employee morale.

One of the major crippling costs of employees walking out is the loss of institutional knowledge, skills, and relationships — within the organization and with customers and partners. The organization also loses the potential value the employee could have delivered. Often succession planning is hampered if you lose a good talent due to office politics. The top performers or those with in-demand skills are often at risk for turnover, even in times of high unemployment.

Organizations that focus on retaining better-experienced employees see significant returns as these professionals are apt to solve complex issues on their own, which benefits the organization. On the same note, replacing an employee carries high costs. After an organization finds qualified employees and successfully recruits and onboards them, the company invests time and resources to train them. Should a new hire leave, all that money goes down the drain. By focusing on employee retention, recruiting costs can be dramatically reduced.

Persistent turnover opens many wrong doors. The most immediate impact is the loss of productivity. On average, it takes a new hire one to two years to reach the productivity of an existing employee. In addition, new hires need time to build relationships with coworkers and customers.

An understaffed environment also causes employee overtime and burnout, lower work quality, and delays. Also, from the customers' perspectives, new employees might take longer to get things done, may be less adept at problem-solving, and be more prone to customer service mistakes. Eventually, this can damage the customer experience. In turn, customers might share their negative experiences, putting the organization's reputation at risk. On the other hand, satisfied employees typically have higher morale and capabilities that shine through when working with customers.

Effective employee retention can save an organization from productivity losses. Engaged employees are more likely to improve customer relationships, and teams that have had time to coalesce also tend to be more productive. Now building such an effective team is a leader's job. And that can happen only if the leader is not blindfolded and is capable of seeing the right talent. Additionally, if you have the right talent within the organization, you must script the succession planning properly. When a high-performer realizes that his talent is considered, his loyalty will be improved, and he will be motivated to produce better results.

It takes significant effort, executive oversight, and targeted investment to create a successful employee retention approach.

However, it pays off for organizations that implement the strategies, tools, and processes required to retain their best and brightest talent. As a leader, if you fail to focus on employee retention, you are going to suffer significant blows not only in terms of the hard costs related to finding, recruiting, onboarding, and training replacements but you will also be challenged with lost productivity and knowledge, impact on customer and employee experiences, and lower morale and fragile corporate culture.

> *"Employees who believe that management is concerned about them as a whole person – not just an employee – are more productive, more satisfied, more fulfilled. Satisfied employees mean satisfied customers, which leads to profitability."*
> — Anne M. Mulcahy

One of the most prominent examples of extracting and grooming the right talent is N. Chandrasekaran. From being a tech trainee to becoming the TATA top guy, his skill has been considered, nurtured, and detected well by the 150-year-old salt-to-sedan behemoth, TATA Group. Chandrasekaran is an alumnus of the Regional Engineering College, Trichy, and joined TCS as in trainee/intern programmer in 1987. He subsequently climbed the ranks to become its CEO.

In October 2016, Chandrasekaran was inducted into the board of Tata Sons, and after the Mistry episode, he was made chairman in January 2017. Under his leadership, the TATA Group now has 26 publicly-listed enterprises with a combined market cap of $314 billion (as of end-2021). In fact, 19 of these 26 listed stocks have outperformed the Nifty since Chandrasekaran took over as the chairman of Tata Sons.

One of his top achievements was winning a bid for Air India. It gave the group back the airline that it had founded and subsequently ceded to the government. Following the acquisition of the Maharaja, TATA now owns three airlines - Tata SIA Airlines, AirAsia India, and Air India. The combined market share of the three now stands at more than 25 percent. Additionally, the stabilization of Tata Motors, which had been battered by competition, is one of his key achievements.

Bringing down Tata Steel's debt and the successful closure of the telecom issue are among the big positives of Chandrasekaran's first tenure.

N. Chandrasekaran is indeed an outsider to the closely-knit Parsi business community. However, Ratan Tata, being a true leader in the truest sense, could never ignore the long list of credentials, Chandrasekaran's dedication toward the company, his undying energy to excel, and, more than anything, Chandrasekaran's alignment with TATA's vision.

A true leader needs a sound talent strategy to extract and retain the right talent from the market. It needs a conscious approach to identify and secure the right talent at the right time to ensure the organization's stable momentum of growth.

A Quick Fact Check

1. **Why should anyone be silent about their performance?**

There is hardly any reason behind the peculiarities of human behavior. Introverts are omnipresent. Not every employee can knock at your door and throw a bouncer for their great performance. It is the leader's job to check on every employee.

2. **If I have to keep an eye on everyone, what is the skip-level manager doing?**

Maybe he is running his own set of rules. Maybe he is a bully, making his juniors slog but stealing their achievements.

3. **How to handle such stealers of performance?**

There is no better way than to be vigilant toward everyone. Too silent employees or too verbose ones are not healthy for the organization. There remains a hidden story behind them. As a leader, you have to bring transparency to the working conditions.

The Silent Killers

Sometimes being a silent worker limit your ability to share your opinions, and in the long run, you fail to make the right impact that you are actually capable of making. Now, why are you a silent worker? Either you just can't or don't want to express yourself. There are some people in the group who contribute more than others, and some are found with awkward silence. While being verbose is not desirable; however, it is important to be able to talk about your work to let the world know about your potential. The tag of Silent Worker seems good until you are tagged as inadequate.

The silent workers always work with the notion of—If I am working, why should I bother about talking about the work I am doing? My leader should take care of this. It is indeed true, but what if the leader is more interested in his own career growth? In that case, why should you leave your destiny completely in the hands of others and stop taking charge of it? The world of business thrives with the formula of $P \times P \times P = Exposure$

1st P is Performance (Silent workers are awesome in that)
2nd P is Projection (Silent workers fail to do so)
3rd P is Perception (Leaders are accountable for that)

If you are a great performer, it is imperative that this is projected with the right sincerity without wearing it on the sleeves. Because that would lead to a perceived connotation resulting in enhanced opportunities for exposure. The workers who are not good at projection tend to lose out in ensuring the penetration of reward. Thus, silence may be good but should not be injurious to your career growth.

Key Takeaways:
- Leadership is about close vigilance
- Scrutinize the outcome, performance and the real performer
- Extract talent and encourage the real talent to exhibit the skills
- Ignorance of the right talent is detrimental to human capital management
- Extracting and exhibiting talent helps in combating employee turnover

PART 3

THE MASTER MODEL BEHIND SUCCESS

7

REAL MOTIVATION STEMS FROM CLARITY

Once upon a time, there lived a king. His huge kingdom had witnessed all the glories of life under his esteemed leadership. As years passed by and the king found himself crippling due to age and ailments, he decided to look for a suitable successor. One who could fit into his shoes perfectly. He sent his two princes in two different directions and asked them to prove their mettle.

The elder prince decided to explore better opportunities in the North while the younger one descended south. A couple of months passed by, and suddenly one night, the king could hear some commotion outside his castle. The younger prince was approaching the castle along with his army of soldiers. Amid that dark night and those raging flambeaus, the old king could perceive their haggard state.

Confused and equally worried, the king rushed down and asked, "Hey, son! Welcome Back. Just wondering about what happened?" The king looked all the more surprised to find some civilians shackled and beaten up amongst the soldiers. He could sense a hint of displeasure amongst the soldier as well.

The young prince smirked and replied, "I couldn't find anything much to do in the south. So, I moved a little toward the west and fought with your enemies there."

The king frowned and cried, "We don't have any enemies in the west."

One of the main soldiers and one captive man exclaimed in chorus. "Well! Now you have."

The night faded out as the king struggled to decide on his younger son's abilities. The next morning brought in a ray of hope as the elder prince returned from his expedition. His army of soldiers looked cheerful. A flicker of hope was kindled as the king welcomed his elder son.

"So, what have you got from the north?" The King asked.

The elder son looked amazed. "Nothing. Was I supposed to get you something? You never told me to do so." The elder prince was intoxicated, and so were the soldiers. None of them looked to have any mission.

The king blinked for a couple of minutes and rephrased his questions. "What did you do in the last few months?"

"Enjoyed." The reply was so prompt that the king could not control his temper. He sat on his throne and decided to disown both the princes for their idiocy and recklessness.

"I had sent you both to prove that you have all the potential to succeed me. Alas! You are good for nothing. One came back after making a new bunch of enemies, and the other just wasted our valuable resources for his own pleasure. How can you ever run this kingdom?" The king shouted at the top of his voice.

The two princes looked confused. The elder one cleared his throat and said, "Father, the other day, you motivated us to go on an expedition to explore life. You never gave us any clear instructions toward any particular job."

"And I was not aware of our friends and foes." The younger one quipped. "How can we judge when we are not given clear-cut instructions about your expectations."

An eerie silence prevailed in the scene. The two princes did seem to be dimwits; however, there lay a major problem with the king's delegation as well.

***

Motivation alone can never create wonders. What if you end up motivating an idiot? The final outcome will be a Motivated Idiot. That's all. A lamebrain can be transformed into a well-informed man only by proper training and significant goal-setting strategies. In this story of the king and his two princes, the king invariably forgot the essentiality of goal-setting. With his motivational speech, he could make the two princes go out of the castle and explore life to become the future king of the kingdom. However, he never taught them what qualities he was looking for while deciding on the future king. And when there was a dearth of basic information, the two princes took the liberty to interpret their own version. Now, whom to be blamed? The two young princes or the king himself?

In my opinion, it was the king's job to guide the two princes in the right direction. His mere words of motivation projected him as a great orator, but the lack of clarity in his words failed the whole endeavor. The situation could have reaped better benefits if only the king could teach the two princes about the whys and hows of succession planning. Let's assume that the king gave the basic pointers to the princes. Does that mean the two princes will end up producing the same outcome? No. Two different individuals are bound to interpret everything differently. However, when the ultimate goal is clear, and the milestone is set, the two princes would have come up with two different, but beneficial ways to produce the desired outcome. Understand the crux of the matter. Interpreting differently but attaining the same goal is far flung from misinterpreting the need. When the king fails to provide clarity about the ultimate goal, the two princes return as aimless as they were before. But if they are given the information about the ultimate goal, they will certainly come back with some concrete results.

Let's assume the king asks the elder son to showcase his administrative skills. The elder son goes and meets the villagers to understand the problem they are facing with the scarcity of water. He then negotiates with the neighboring kingdom to open the dam to combat the drought. In return, the neighboring kingdom is given a portion of the harvest. Similarly, the king asks the younger son to explore some of the unclaimed lands in the vicinity to see if their kingdom can be expanded. The younger son takes a team of geologists and other scholars and comes back with detailed information. The demography, culture, land quality, mineral deposition, etc. He chalks out the best encroachment plan in a direction that will fetch maximum benefits to the kingdom in terms of resources.

Now, tell me if you think the two princes are dimwits. No individual is utterly an idiot if given proper direction to perform. Performance potential is determined by the degree of clarity of goals. The clearer your target is, the more determined the performance will be. Of course, it is a Catch-22 kind of situation, and the whole process runs in the loop of Inspiration–Motivation–Action. Still, mere motivation can never translate into action. Leaders have to be clear about the bull's eye. Once the bull's eye is set, the performers will somehow find out a way to put the dart accurately. They may falter initially, but with repeated action, results come in handy.

> *"Effective leaders don't have to be passionate. They don't have to be charming. They don't have to be brilliant…They don't have to be great speakers. What they must be is clear. Above all else, they must never forget the truth that of all the human universals – our need for security, community, clarity, authority, and for respect— our need for clarity… is the most likely to engender in our confidence, persistence, resilience, and creativity."*
> — Marcus Buckingham

The strongest pillar of organizational culture is organizational clarity. Probably, the biggest competency of a leader is designed by the kind of clarity he holds.

Clearness of goal, lucidity in action as well as direction and simplicity as to perception or understanding, and complete freedom from indistinctness or ambiguity are some of the essential qualities of a leader who wishes to build a high-performing team. Organizational clarity is the greatest strategic advantage for any organization. Conceived as strategy, embodied by leadership, and delivered by teams, clarity scripts the bottom line of every desirable result.

Now, there are six basic questions: who, what, when, where, why, and how that the leader must define while crafting the goal strategy. A sheer absence of clarity on these questions nourishes confusion about expectations and mistrust. It, in turn, impacts results and meddles with the speed at which an organization reaches its target.

Let's understand the crux of the matter with this hypothetical case. Vincent is the sales team leader and gets a new bunch of recruits for the newly launched product X of the company. Well-mannered, always approachable, and encouraging, he calls the new recruits and motivates them to deliver a 5% increase in sales. The new recruits are given a list of praiseworthy words without even performing anything to reach the target.

Anyway, ambiguity runs riot as the new recruits are not told about who is the target market and what are the current needs. They go into the market and try hard to sell product X, only to be trapped in more confusion. Some come to the conclusion that the launch timing is not right as they fail to find any demand in the market. At the same time, another bunch of people fails to understand how to persuade customers to buy X. Some keep knocking at the wrong target audience, while others feel demotivated in the absence of clear instructions.

In the end, leave alone an increase in sales, the team could not even meet the basic target. Vincent is saddened as it casts a bad reputation for his team without realizing the root of the problem. The top leader comes down the ladder to scrutinize the issue with the sales team. As the leader opens the communication barrier, the new recruits could raise their concern openly.

Each one of them seems to be an excellent communicator with efficient sales skills; however, they failed because they were not given a clear-cut demonstration of the six basic questions of performance. This time, Vincent answers every question regarding the target market, product details, past strategies, etc., and sends his team back. In a month's time, the company could fetch a 7% increase in sales.

In this case, Vincent was never wrong the first time. But he was only partially right while disposing of a half-baked strategy. His words of motivation let his team come to the office every day but couldn't make them work toward the desired target. However, as he detailed everything, he did not spoon-feed the course of action. Instead, he guided the team in the right direction with more clarity.

The clarity in the course of action is essential. Let's say you train a monkey to beat someone. You snatch the essence of fear from it and ask the monkey to beat a lion. It doesn't know anything about the lion and goes to beat it with a stick. Now, as the monkey is motivated enough to do the job, it indeed goes into action. But fails to strategize. The lion is big and more powerful, and the monkey is given just a stick; the strength of the stick is unknown to the monkey. In no time, the stick breaks, and the lion also pounces on the monkey.

It is a classic example to demonstrate a failed endeavor of any organization. If the leader ends his role with a motivational speech, the team is prepared to get out and perform, but they will be ignorant about what to perform and how to perform efficiently. Motivation is quite like a sugar rush. It hits hard, makes you feel infused with all the enthusiasm, and then suddenly sends you crashing back to earth once the intoxication vanishes.

If you pay close attention, you will find that motivation works out through the narration of heroic stories, motivational quotes, and inspirational speeches. They are like the sugar cubes you would feed a donkey to make it walk. Can you make it reach the destination? No. You have to whip it or push it harder. Clarity of goals is that push every employee needs to move closer to the target.

Now, clarity includes a variety of communication. In an organizational setup, the leaders have to chalk out strategic clarity. While planning on a particular project, it may seem like the leader and the team are on the same page while the reporting happens on paper.

However, things may turn upside down as soon as personal interpretation is put forth. Even in the bigger format, as they get in a room together and openly discuss core strategies around organizational mission and values, you can find the knowledge gap. A lack of alignment and clarity is the most common problem any organization faces. Very often, organizational clarity remains restricted only to the top few levels of the hierarchy who have developed both the tools and the talents for overall organizational growth. But then, it is like keeping a piece of information only inside the brain. Until the brain transmits the signal, how the other organs can function?

Running an organization to reap profitable goals is nothing less than a battle. Every individual member must be aligned with the goal of winning the battle. The process of chalking out a winning plan involves three crucial steps.

1. **A clear and simple mission where the expected outcome is well-defined**. That is the answer to where, when, and why behind a step yet to be taken. #
2. **Clarity regarding the professional competency and character of the team**. It is about placing the right people at the right job. #
3. **Imparting clarity about the culture of the organization**. A target can be reached in many ways; however, the employees must be clear about the ethics, values, and norms of the organization. In one of his interviews, Ratan Tata said, "they say in India, you have to bribe to get to the top. Never in my life have I paid a bribe or gratification to anyone." And that is what is called organizational culture.#

If I throw some light on the Edtech sector, although every startup is basically integrating a new or advanced version of technology, no one can meddle with the core concept of the subject. While launching a new product in the market, as a leader, I do have to entertain the prevailing challenges as described by my customers. Until I understand WHERE and WHY is the knowledge gap and WHEN is the right time to launch the solution, I can never let my best men work on a new product. Additionally, it is necessary to tailor-make the right team to solve any problem. Diverse skills, fresh perspectives, and competitive edge must be entertained. And lastly, as a leader, I must dictate the company norms and ethics to my team.

The team should not cross the ethical boundaries of the company to crack a deal. Organizational clarity is crucial because it forms the foundation of empowerment.

The business environment is moving at high speed, so much so that the organization hardly gets time for excessive contemplation and waiting. Every organization now needs to be agile, which in turn can be created by having a clear and simple mission, creating a workforce with desired competence, and building a culture of shared values and norms. You have to understand that clarity is often synonymous with simplicity. As a leader, when you make short, clear statements about your defined customers, core strengths, desired future, and action plans, you prevent employees from falling into the trap of confusion and anxiety. Your clarity of thought, in turn, kindles confidence throughout the team and replaces uncertainty with resilience and creativity. Additionally, the quality of clarity is also an essential element for leading large groups of diverse employees toward an optimum future.

> *"With leadership accounting for 15 percent of an organization's success, we need to truly understand its fundamental principles, how to identify those who demonstrate it and how to nurture its traits in their potential successors."*
> — Warren Bennis

When every organization is unique with its opportunities and challenges, every leader is bound to have a unique style statement.

However, a successful leader has certain key ingredients for growth:

- A guiding vision
- Passion

- Integrity (that includes self-awareness, candor, and maturity)
- Curiosity
- Emotional self-control
- Transparency
- Building human connection

A great leader must be capable of discovering the right talent for the optimum strategy and must capitalize on the growth. In any case, whether it is within an organization or in other aspects of life, humans are scared of uncertainty. You cannot motivate an engineering aspirant to clear the IIT entrance without guiding him about the course details. An IIT aspirant cannot clear the exam by watching motivational speeches of IIT alumni.

Similarly, an employee cannot reach the said target if he harbors uncertainty in his mind. Amongst all the universal fears and needs, the most dreadful fear the leaders confront is the fear of the future. In this constantly changing market scenario, leaders are challenged by the unknown; therefore, it is all the more difficult to design clear goals.

Even with a strong ego and optimism, leaders can never escape complexities and uncertainties. Their success depends on finding a way to engage employees' fears of the unknown and renovating them into a strong-willed commitment to a vision for a better future. Leaders must define the future in vivid terms because clarity is the antidote to anxiety, and thus they should utilize it to get the optimum benefits. As a leader, you have to focus on four key areas to ensure clarity in action:

Whom do you serve?

How can you define your customers based on what they want from your company? Now, these answers can be obtained with sufficient fieldwork. Compiling information from customers enables you to craft the real picture of your customer base. And as you understand your customer, your employees can visualize clients and understand their concerns and values well and can take suitable actions without your regular intervention.

What is our core strength?

When you define your organization's core strength, you educate your employees about their competitive edge in the market. As a leader implants confidence in core strengths, anxiety is replaced by the resilience and a zeal to reach the target. As Marcus Buckingham states: *"The strengths you pick don't have to reflect current reality. You don't have to be right. You just have to be clear. It is also essential that your people believe that you believe they can excel in the ways you've defined."* What is the core score?

Every employee holds different skills but with different magnitudes. One who is good at communication skills may not have much technical competency. To ensure clarity of goals, leaders should avoid measuring all the skills at once. The core score of an employee must be determined based on the skill that is needed exclusively for the work at hand.

What should be today's course of action?

Two kinds of actions happen in an organization. Symbolic action – It occurs when a particular goal is achieved to create confidence and success. Systematic action – It includes new activities that focus on the needs of customers, highlight core strengths, and lead to success on core metrics. Now, understand that embedding clarity in day-to-day operations requires focus and discipline.

While some people are innately clear with their purpose, the leader must incorporate discipline and practice. While motivation can get only 10% job done, leaders have to follow a few steps to induce clarity in thought and action. Motivating is easier because it is verbose; however, imparting clarity to the team needs better efforts from the leader.

Are your words aligned with actions?

Retrospection is one of the common habits of great leaders. It helps leaders to sift through the clutter, define essentials and focus on what really matters. As a leader, your words, actions, and choices have the ability to influence the team. So, choose your heroes judiciously. Let's say you recognize a high-performer, and then you should be explicit in your recognition by explaining how he could serve your defined customer, his core strength, how he met or exceeded your core metric, and the actions he took to bring the desired future one step closer. On the same note, when you discipline yourself to practice using your words, images, and stories in a particular way, it helps employees perceive the future with clarity. Remember, the best leaders need not come up with newer and better speeches, but they do need to have a grasp of the present reality and should utter the pertinent things. An organization's core goal doesn't change drastically every now and then. So, the leader must discipline in refining the descriptions of the future goal as and when the situation demands.

Motivation can infuse some confidence, but with clarity, leaders can provoke persistence, resilience, and creativity.

Motivating a group to act in cohesion toward the same goal is indeed a complex and nuanced process. It requires understanding and perseverance to get it right. However, what happens if the leader relies on fallacies or misconceptions? Leaders often bask under the influence of several myths that surround the concept of motivation.

Myth 1: The whole team can be motivated using the same tactic.
Reality Check: Every individual has a unique perspective and motivational needs.

Let's consider two individuals from the same sales team. Thomas is inherently motivated because he has always wanted to be in sales. He has great communication skills and a willingness to explore untouched domains, and he is already clear about the ultimate mission. On the other hand, Rashmi has been working in the company for a couple of years now and still feels a little disjointed from the goal. Although she has great communication skills, she is not inclined to sales. This job is a mere source of income, and she is always looking for a change. In fact, given a chance, she would like to go to the customer service department.

Now, can they both be motivated to reach the sales target in the same way? No. In fact, Thomas will not need a motivational speech. He will just need clarity about the desired sales target. At the same time, the leader has to encourage Rashmi to focus her vision on the whole concept of sales first. An individual's motivational profile is a lot like a fingerprint. It is indeed true that people are motivated by a finite list of factors; there prevails an infinite number of combinations when it comes to these factors' relative importance to that person. Statistically, there are about 7.5 quadrillion different possible motivational profiles; thus, the chances of two people having the exact same motivational needs are quite remote.

Myth 2: HR motivates, and the team works wonders
Reality Check: The C-suite, HR and line managers, and even the colleague sitting inside the next cubicle has a role to play in creating motivating workplaces.

Motivation is not magic. There is no magic wand with which a leader can hypnotize the team to produce optimum results. Consider a case of sudden technological intervention within a team. Let's say the internal communications department, which basically works on the principles of content creation, is now asked to update all the projects in an app like ZOHO. Most of the team members are young, and they are habituated to such apps; however, two older employees find it difficult to incorporate this change. In this case, the goal is clear — uploading and updating every work on the online portal; however, the process is not. Now, an HR motivating those two employees will not fetch any result because there prevails a knowledge gap that can be bridged by those younger colleagues. Sometimes, along with motivation and clarity, cooperation and collaboration play a major role.

Myth 3: Rewards motivate
Reality Check: Employees are motivated from within

According to the classic carrot and stick approach to management, rewards and punishments are key to motivation. By keeping bonuses, incentives, and extra holidays on the one hand and criticism, disciplinary actions, and dismissal on the other, management allure employees toward performance.

Such an approach constitutes extrinsic motivation. However, there is something called intrinsic motivation, which is composed of the values and preferences that drive a person from within and make them do a particular task. Going by the previous example, Thomas has the intrinsic motivation, while Rashmi is working because of extrinsic motivation. Intrinsic Motivation is strongly linked to increased engagement, better performance, and overall happiness.

Myth 4: Motivated individuals can be easily managed.
Reality Check: High motivation kindles high needs

Thomas is highly motivated to increase the sales revenue for the company. He is inclined to do some market research and finds out about an emerging feature in the market. In no time, he contacted the higher-ups and requested this new implementation to make the company ahead in the market.

However, the resource allocation and finance department opine otherwise due to budgetary constraints. Thomas's endeavor, though, is appreciated, but it couldn't be implemented. Now, Thomas feels ditched without realizing that although his intention is beneficial for the organization, there are other factors involved, like human resources, financial upheavals, structural needs, etc.

An organization needs to balance out every aspect. Thomas, in turn, showcases how the new technological feature can help the company cut on human resources.

Now, that suggestion comes as a cultural shock for the whole management because it is beyond the company's values and ethics.

In this scenario, a highly motivated individual developed special needs because he could sense the dearth of motivated employees around him. It induced a sense of supremacy that became difficult to manage. Although Thomas was clear with the organizational goals, he never had clarity over the organization's culture, values, and ethics.

> *"It is the lack of clarity that creates chaos and frustration. Those emotions are poison to any living goal."*
> — Steve Maraboli

When a team designed to work together toward a common goal has clarity, and everyone has a clear understanding of everything about the work required to effectively achieve their goal, their performance index is enhanced. Every team member must answer a few questions before indulging in the said task. What is the goal, and how to reach the target? Is there a strategy well chalked out? As a member of this team, what is my exact role to play? How much authority do I have to make a decision? Now, answers to all these questions can make clarity the default state of mind for the team. However, it doesn't work like this. Instead of clarity, chaos and confusion are the default companion of every team. Moving teams from chaos to clarity is one of the most vital functions of leadership.

Commonly, leaders tend to overestimate how much clarity their team has because everything is already clear in their own heads. On the other hand, employees tend not to surface the need for more clarity as it is embarrassing to admit that you're not sure what you're supposed to be doing—or why. There are three kinds of clarity that need to be explained. Clarity of purpose, clarity of plan, and clarity of responsibility. Here's why each is important and some concrete steps to achieve them.

It is essential to start with a WHY. For one member, working toward a particular goal is just a practical option, while for others, it may not be. For example, a marketer with clarity on their customer's goals will more effectively empathize with the audience. An engineer with clarity on the market trend can make performance tradeoffs that optimize the customer experience. Similarly, a VP with clarity on the company's unique mission and vision will stay focused on the most important initiatives instead of getting distracted by other potential opportunities or competitors. A team that truly understands and believes in a common goal can persevere through difficult challenges.

If you are leading a team that is part of a larger organization, you have to help everyone on your team understand how the larger organization is impacting the world, how your team is critical to the success of the organization, and how their individual work is important to the success of the team. You would have succeeded in achieving clarity of purpose when everyone on your team can answer these two questions: "If we're wildly successful, how will the world be different?" and "How is the work you're doing now directly contributing to that success?"

Continuing the same tone, you have to understand that with clarity of purpose, the team knows the destination, but with clarity of plan, the team knows how to get there. The plan you co-create with your team defines the current best understanding of how best to achieve the mission of the team. The clarity of the plan is essentially a pyramid, with every layer progressively more detailed.

If you're leading a whole company or division, your pyramid should look like this:

- **Mission:** This is your raison d'etre for the foreseeable future. Everyone on the team should know this by heart. For example, Tesla's mission is to accelerate the world's transition to sustainable energy.
- **Strategy:** A concise explanation of the high-level approach you're taking to achieve the mission.
- **Objectives:** This includes short-term goals (one year) and is ideally measurable.
- **Key results**: These are shorter-term (e.g., one-quarter) goals. Key results should be sure for measurable.

- **Projects:** Smaller missions that an individual team undertakes to achieve the key result. For example, execute a nationwide marketing campaign to launch an additional feature in the product.
- **Tasks:** These are the individual steps that need to be taken in order to execute the project.

If any one member falls out of the loop, the whole system can crumble. Nevertheless, to combat that, clarity of responsibility is needed. In management terms, there prevails a general rule; each item should have exactly one owner. When no one is responsible for something, it doesn't get done. When two or more people share responsibility for the same task or objective, the whole broth may be spoiled as they may end up stepping on each other's toes. As a leader, it is your responsibility not only to create clarity for the present time but to be vigilant as time goes on in unearthing a plethora of ways when your team loses clarity.

The faster an organization grows in size, the more complex the work grows. And that's when it becomes even more critical to have clarity. Clarity improves a team's ability to execute and change directions confidently and its overall satisfaction. However, it would be foolish to get addicted to clarity.

When change is the only constant, you are bound to face ambiguity at some point in time. A team that freezes in the face of ambiguity can never get very far in navigating uncharted territories. The more entrepreneurial a team is, the more comfortable it should be with ambiguity. There is never a perfect definition of clarity or motivation. As a leader, the more you learn, the more you train your team, and the better clarity they get. And once clarity of purpose, plan and individual responsibility is bestowed upon the team, each member is automatically motivated to perform well.

Tête-à-Tête With Failure

Sony Walkman; is a tale of a grandiose launch and miserable failure. After the sale of the 400 million Walkman music player, the death though seemed untimely, but it was never unforeseen. Walkman's miserable loss proved that even in the space of innovation, there is a dire need for clarity as to which way to proceed.

In 1979, Walkman came into the market of music lovers as the big bang. It maintained a stronghold for two decades. However, the dawn of the 21st century witnessed its failure to withstand the market of change. Why did Sony Walkman fail? Did people stop listening to music, or did Sony fail to fathom the essence of innovation? Neither was true. Sony did churn out innovation with the advent of CD players.

Instead of being a victim, Sony took advantage of it and successfully released Walkman's CD version to sustain Walkman's market position. However, the team failed to have a clear perspective about successive thrusts to innovation. The team was motivated and technically sound but never had the clarity of the future probability of further advancement. With the growing popularity of the Internet and the option of downloading music to MP3 players, Walkman faced the biggest disruption. As the team never anticipated such a drastic change, they were not clear about producing a stronger response. Subsequently, Walkman walked into a vacuum in the innovation space with a dearth of clear goals. Apple desperately took advantage of it and responded with iPod. If one listened to the technological gurus, iPod nurtured a sustaining innovation that everyone expected Sony to deliver.

Key Takeaways:

- Mere motivation cannot translate into action
- Clarity of goals is essential for individual as well as organizational growth.
- Clarity of purpose, clarity of plan, and clarity of responsibility; all three must be explained
- Organizational clarity forms the foundation of empowerment
  - Motivation encourages, clarity enables

8

IDEATION TO EXECUTION

Can you believe that the board of directors called Steve Jobs crazy for entering the cell phone domain? They all found the space already saturated enough to bear any fruit for the long and laborious effort. Was Jobs crazy? On the day of the iPhone launch, every second newspaper underlined only one line, and It *Doesn't Work*. As of 2022, the US has 113 million iPhone users, while there are over a billion users worldwide. So, did it not work? Was Steve Jobs crazy? Probably yes. He was crazy enough to trade with an existing idea but with a unique twist. How? Because he knew that every idea could bear the sweet fruit of success only if executed strategically. His ideology and leadership revolve around acting and building rather than mere ruling.

There would have been a couple of times that you were in a meeting, and your innovative idea is appreciated. Your peers, stakeholders, and even the team members would have commented — You got a great idea, and you should turn it into reality. But what typically happens? Most of the time, you sleep over your idea pondering over all the probable hiccups and hurdles.

Most of the great ideas never see the dawn of execution, either due to a lack of courage and the right resources or due to the dearth of clarity toward the course of execution. An idea can be hatched at any point in time, and that is the essentiality of entrepreneurship. You walk through your routine and suddenly encounter a problem, and your brain starts connecting the dots to seek a solution. Eventually, you hatch a fantastic idea for a product that was never thought of before, and voila! You cross the first step of ideation. But then, the most critical question knocks at your doorstep. How do you build the product? You know about the problem prevailing in the market and can effectively locate the right spot to grow your business in this untouched domain. Your idea seems to be believable; however, is it executable? Another added prick to the question is; do you have enough clarity about how to proceed in the course of execution?

Hatching a wonderful idea is more like kindling motivation. However, as stated earlier, mere motivation is like a punctured tire. It can exist in a vehicle but doesn't hold any significance. It never helps the vehicle to go ahead in the journey. Consider your car broke in the middle of the road. You are aware of the problem that you cannot reach your destination without repairing it. The problem is known, and so the solution is. Now, do you see a mechanic nearby? Or can you google about a mechanic? Realizing the need for a mechanic is clarity. No matter where you stand in your leadership pursuit, you have to envision the complete process of transforming an idea into execution. Any unprepared or underprepared effort can ruin even the greatest of ideas.

One of the classic examples of inefficient execution is the dramatic failure of Compaq. Improper execution occurred at every hierarchical level. During the 80s and '90s, Compaq was a flourishing PC brand, and it could create the first successful and fully legal IBM PC clone. It set a record as a startup, so much so that IBM was seized from being the standard-bearer in the PC market. Compaq drew attention to making sturdy, highly regarded PCs and servers.

However, now Compaq has transformed into a trademark that HP owns but never uses. Compaq's failure reflects upon a miasma of unplanned and underprepared execution.

If we dig deeper, Compaq rose to dominance through its price war strategies against IBM and other early PC manufacturers. However, once it reached the leadership positions, Compaq executives moved to an ill-strategized wave of change as they believed in the need to out-innovate their competitors to retain the top position. Apparently, they went to make some acquisitions that never worked out. In 1997, their acquisition of Tandem Computers, a mainframe computer maker, for $3 billion and of DEC in 1998 for $9.6 billion turned out to be a waste of significant resources.

Similarly, the DEC merger failed to bear fruit as DEC was in the business of manufacturing computer chips when Compaq never had any plans to continue in that line of business. Moreover, DEC's chips were not compatible with Compaq computers. Another major issue cropped up with this merger — a clash of company culture. Staff was demotivated by the huge layoffs. A hostile working environment further led to missed deadlines and an inability to shift large quantities of inventory. In short, the business was on the path to ruins.

The top management, too, went down the hole as a series of scandals forced various executives out in 1999. Compaq's computer sales dropped in 1999 even though the Y2K issue reinforced good sales of computer equipment. Compaq somehow failed to capitalize on the opportunity as there were too many things on its plate. To retain good faith with its subsidiary divisions, the company took refuge in a hands-off approach and paved a path toward decline as productivity was compromised. An ill-executed marketing strategy that shifted from price to premium products led to the hiring of a network of middlemen sellers who had to assist with the price war strategy. All of a sudden, they were instructed to sell premium devices with value-adding services, which they didn't have any expertise or experience in. On the same note, the leaders sitting on the top thought of minting money by leasing out unrealistic sales targets to those middlemen sellers. Based on the set target, huge sales figures were promised to stock owners, and huge inventories were created, which the company struggled to shift, contributing to its decline. Now, with huge targets set and huge sales figures promised, the huge inventories created were manufactured with loosened standards resulting in poor-quality products. Eventually, customers started to skip Compaq computers. Over a period of time, the middlemen sellers realized the lukewarm response in the market. And to avoid handling after-sales services and customer complaints, they started overselling the product. This attitude was unethical, but it slowly permeated through every layer of the company.

Along with the dot-com burst, the market was flooded with surplus equipment, and Compaq had to compete with its own product until the market absorbed the surplus. Now, Intel had started producing chipsets and motherboards, and Compaq's rival could outsource their engineering needs to Intel at a cheaper cost. The top management brought another mishap through inventory mismanagement. Dell could outcompete because of its superior inventory management with computers made to order and just-in-time delivery. By 2001, HP ruled on the top position while Compaq's cash reserves went into a dangerous state. A swap stock merger happened; however, due to a temperament clash, some high-profile resignations took place in Compaq, which razed the company to operate on the whims of HP. There is no dearth of reasons behind a business' failure. At every stage, wherever Compaq stumbled, you can find a sheer misalignment with execution strategy. Whether it was the idea of big acquisitions or shifting toward premium products, there prevailed an ill-planned strategy. Top management struggling with business ethics, middle management resorting to shortcut solutions, sheer ignorance toward the concept of customer satisfaction, and many such threads joined to produce the ultimate noose of complete failure.

Ideation to execution is a long and laborious process. Whether the idea is about building a new product or ideating about a novel marketing strategy, converting an idea into a reality is never an easy task. When you step into the shoes of leadership, giving life to ideas is no less than giving birth to a child. One of the major quirks is no one will ever understand your idea or the dynamics associated with it as you do. Similarly, there is no set rule to decipher what is needed mentally, physically, and intellectually to effectively execute an idea. The process of executing an idea into a reality is a never-ending cycle if you, as a leader, want to keep that idea alive over changing times. A leader's job is to keep the company and its product sustainable in the market. And to do so, there is a need for constant innovation in product design, validation and testing procedures, marketing strategy, etc.

A company founded on the premise of a great idea may go into a dungeon if they fail to innovate in its execution plans in changing market scenario. For example, Shree Shakti Enterprises opened three new manufacturing units, expanded the company's workforce to 500, and increased its turnover from Rs 10 crore to Rs 140 crore from 2010 to 2019 under the effective leadership of Rahul Bajaj. Their growth seemed steady, with an average of 40 percent yearly. However, the Covid pandemic scripted a different fate, and Shree Shakti had to close all its manufacturing units. Consumption fell drastically, and sales of non-essential items hit bottom. Instead of bogging down, the management decided to innovate as a survival strategy, and the company started building products that could come in handy in the present crisis. From sensor-based sanitizer dispensers to hands-free hand wash systems and automatic foot sanitizers, Shree Shakti ventured into uncharted territory.

If you see around, there are umpteen examples of strategic execution that have led a company to come out of impending doom. Innovation, followed by effective execution, is the ultimate mantra. It has a significant role to play even in workforce management. There are cases when the workforce is not innovative enough and are just trained and wired only to execute what they are told to do. Essentially, they are most proficient at completing short-term, immediate tasks. On the other hand, employees are least proficient at multiplying the opportunities that lie hidden in the initial task they were asked to complete.

What should a leader do in such situations? You conceive an idea, chalk out an effective plan for your team to execute, and eventually, they all become your ardent follower and do not put any extra thought while encountering a problem in due course of time. In another scenario, the team just fails to comprehend your idea and no execution takes place.

For an organization to remain competitive in the market, ideation to effective execution must happen at every level of the hierarchy. And as a leader, you have to accept the fact that no one can read your vision until you lead the whole team. There prevails a long background story before a product actually comes into the market. From the discovery of the scope to build a new product to designing the product, marketing it, and commercializing it, a leader has to design a series of realistic milestones for the team. The success boils down to only one question – how well does the team understand the leader's thoughts and actions?

Over the years, different management gurus and strategy planners have proposed a sequence of steps to turn an idea into a fool-proof product. Nevertheless, the core essence remained the same. An idea undergoes a chain of events; from conception to execution while treading over several trials and errors with product designing, customer and market validation, and commercialization. Effective planning is the crucial element that links every step. Transforming any idea into a fruitful outcome is a laborious task and without proper planning, efficient execution becomes impossible.

To understand it better, let's dig a little deeper into the product development lifecycle to understand the sheer need for strategic and well-planned execution. From the management perspective, any product that comes into the market goes through the following five steps:

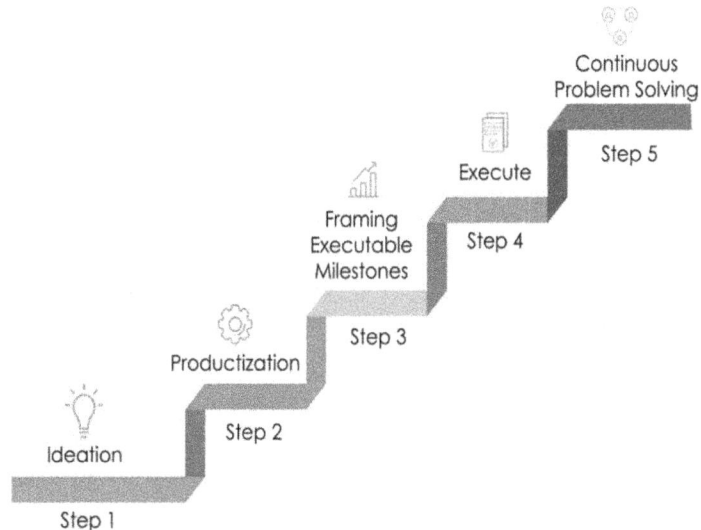

From ideation to execution, at every stage, the leader sets a milestone, while the decisive factor is how executional and realistic the milestone is. For example, Compaq's sales target was unrealistic to reap any benefit.

As a leader, you have to be on your toes to solve every problem that comes at a different stage of the product life cycle. Right from ideation, you and your team will be attacked by a myriad of challenges; be it volatility of the market or absurdity of your idea or it can be as worse as internal organizational conflict through resource allocation.

However, amid all the challenges, leaders have to strategize every course of action from the pre-ideation stage till execution while embracing a problem-solving approach throughout. Let's have a detailed analysis of the various stages along with the problems that are encountered and how leaders can solve them effectively.

Ideation

The dawn of ideation starts at the discovery phase, where you actively seek out information about the market trends, rising demands amongst the customers, and every other element that demands a change or an introduction of a new idea or product. Let's assume you are an entrepreneur, and you want to move ahead with time before your existing business proposal goes into the doldrums. How do you proceed?

The most accepted route is by asking open-ended questions to the customer base. The goal is to collect and collate customers' feedback and the market scenario into a meaningful form so that you can come up with a probable solution. In this pre-ideation or discovery phase, you get a fair list of problems and struggles that your potential market is currently experiencing.

Additionally, you understand your customers' persona, which will help you focus on prototypes within your market in later phases. Discovery is followed by the phase of ideation, where you actually start thinking critically about what you have fathomed from your potential customers and the market. It is a critical stage while making assumptions about the customers, market, and solution. You and your team must produce testable hypotheses around these assumptions. Now, as often found, the hypotheses you hatch or the assumptions you throw at your team might not get accepted easily. The team that actually works on the ground might make you aware of the wide array of risks involved with the idea. Secondly, if you are proposing a drastic disruption in the normal course of product designing, your team may fail to comprehend or may even oppose the whole proposition.

How do you manage such conflict? Can you make your team visualize your version? Let's assume you have been a very efficient communicator and can persuade anybody. Does that mean you will succeed every time with every plan of yours? Doubtful. Your team that works at the ground level is more competent with the stark reality of the market.

Your sales department is more aware of customers' perceptions and loyalty toward your brand and other brands. There is a high probability that your team doesn't approve of your new idea. Secondly, what if the team is ready, but your investors are hesitant? This is where the testable hypotheses come into the picture.

Productization

At this stage, the design team comes together and builds a prototype of the product and instigate the second stage called, productization. This is essentially to check if the assigned milestone can be executed or not. Eventually, the prototype enters into an iterative process. The product is to be tested in the market, which will lead to more discovery and more ideation. To avoid falling prey to analysis-paralysis, you have to start developing your MVP. The leader's role turns crucial here as the team is going to face the hardest problem during this phase. As a leader, you have to constantly nudge the problem and solve it to remain viable in this discovery-ideation-confirmation loop.

Moreover, the viability of your product is also under close scrutiny by your other stakeholders. In the end, the challenges that you face at this phase give you the complete SWOT analysis of your performance as a leader, your team's competency in the market, and your product's viability as well. Eventually, you enter the stage where you know which segment to prioritize. You get a reality check that not every milestone that you could set is executable.

Framing Executable Milestone

"Strategy equals execution. All the great ideas and visions in the world are worthless if they can't be implemented rapidly and efficiently. Good leaders delegate and empower others liberally, but they pay attention to details every day".
— Colin Powell

As a leader, you now have to prioritize a number of metrics like customer value, technical acceptability, and competitive advantage. Whatever tops the chart must be validated with your customer base. Once it is done, you and your team are ready to design the final product. Once you have got your priority straight, you can chalk out your course of action with much clarity. Essentially, you take all the data and start piecing together the technical definition that can help your team to work out. There lingers a cautionary note and you shouldn't start designing something until you know that your conceptualization of the final product is aligned with the customer's viewpoint. Every idea can be visualized in multiple ways, and thus, your conceptualization as a creator may be far-flung from how and what the actual target audience needs.

A lot of product management teams end up wasting time and energy on designing a particular product specification that the customer base never wanted. As a leader, you have to foresee your product's viability for the next 6 to 12 months initially, for technology and the market is constantly evolving. In essence, your ideation to execution journey has many onlookers; the core team, investors, and of course, your customer. Even if your team is okay with your proposal, does your customer base comply with your idea?

Moreover, the execution of an idea cannot take place in a vacuum. As a leader, involving your UX team, architecture team, marketing and support team, and even your development teams in the design process are essential to reap better success. The sooner you approve or disprove the feasibility of your solution, the least resources you will waste. Also, the more people you involve in the design phase, the easier it is to manage expectations during the implementation phase. In the end, you get the specifications necessary to hand something over to the development team to actually build.

Execute

Execution is the stage where the rubber meets the road.

It is the stage where most people focus on showcasing their actual potential. It is like actually getting into the field and facing real-life challenges. The crux is to understand that the goal is not about delivering the product the team has designed. Rather, the actual point is to deliver a valuable solution to customers' problems. If the customer proposes a better way to handle the problem, it is your duty to reconsider your whole ideation stage. After all, the market is run by demands and not by your fantasy. As a leader, you must sacrifice your egos on the altar of customer empowerment whenever the situation demands.

At this point in time, your team is delivering at a regular pace while touching every milestone. However, is it enough to build a finished product? Does the process of execution stop there? Releasing a finished product in the market is a continuous process. Implementation and launching of a product walk on parallel tracks.

Let's assume you are the product manager. You have to ensure that the marketing and sales team understand the problems that the product is solving. Additionally, every member in the field must know the value that the product is adding to the customers' life. The sales team often makes the mistake of selling the features instead of value. Have you ever wondered about the marketing strategy of iPhones? It is essentially a smartphone, but the company does not sell the features but the value the phone instills in one's life. iPhone is marketed as a prestige symbol. Similarly, Oppo or Vivo phones market the value of capturing precious moments through their highly-advanced camera.

It is perpetually the leader's job to let the team understand the true value of the product and teach them how to sell the value instead of features. The team working as a direct interface with the customer must know the product as well as its value in the present market. As a leader, if you fail to describe the feature/benefit breakdown to your field worker, you are either not working on the right thing or you haven't placed the right strategy for implementation.

The leader must be aware of the marketing and sales team's go-to-market strategy is, so that they can provide the necessary feedback and supporting information for them to achieve success in launching your product in the market.

Let's assume your product is launched in the market. People are buying; customers seem to be happy; your sales team is reaching the set target, and so on. Does that mean your role as a leader has stopped? Sustainment is the biggest goal. As a leader, you need to ensure that the technical sales teams, support teams, and even the internal services teams are working in close association. One of the crucial steps of execution is to hear the customers' feedback. There is a high chance that you and your design team have slipped through the cracks. And there again, your discovery cycle takes a new plunge. In the end, you, as a leader, are bestowed with a new set of information, ideas, and problems to innovate further and enter into a new product lifecycle.

My chase against execution problems came to a halt regarding the complexity of our recently launched product. We had launched the integrated system in education. Earlier, people used to have different vendors to serve different purposes. It was like books were purchased from one while Enterprise Resource Planning (ERP) used to be purchased from somebody, smartboard came from another vendor, and the training used to be purchased from somebody else. So, it was like a different segment of running a school was obtained from different sources. Our organization came up with the idea of integrating everything under the same roof. We provided books and workbooks, and along came ERP, training, and a tablet.

However, the challenge was big because every segment of my product had a different competitor. When I opened books, our product was compared with the publishers, and a similar comparison worked out with ERP as well. There was absolutely no room to escape this comparison, so we had a placeholder. Instead of holding training sessions with half-hearted participants, we decided on a placeholder on the table. We just moved with publicizing the core idea of providing an integrated system.

The moment the term integrated could grab the audience's attention, we showcased the slides in which they were interested. Of course, we had a wonderful marketing strategy in place, and most of the audience invariably ended up asking for more information. Showing books, workbooks, and our unique way of integration could make us stand apart from the competition.

This strategy worked wonders as a lot of time was saved on negotiation and explanation. The service was tailor-made according to the customers' requirements. The more they elaborated their demands, the more scope we got to ideate further and improve our product further.

With competition thriving at every corner, ideation seems to be a very small step before the gigantic approach one has to take during the execution process. Developing a product holds a different course of execution as all the strategies are to be chalked out inside the organizational wall. A more complex approach to execution occurs at the last stage of product development. Executing a fool-proof marketing plan is a way more laborious task.

When a product enters the market, its progression happens through 5 distinct stages—development, introduction, growth, maturity, and decline. From the launch to the eventual withdrawal of the product from the market, the leader must strategize different execution plans according to the placement of the product in the market. The leader must use the product life cycle to execute strategic decisions about pricing, expansion into new markets, packaging design, and more.

Continuous Problem-Solving Approach

Making informed decisions is one of the major challenges. There prevails a list of problems:

- Have you planned to increase ROI on product launches?
- What is your strategy to increase company profitability?
- Are you proactive in tweaking marketing messages to stay connected with targeted audiences?
- Have you planned ahead to maintain and improve product appeal, reputation, and customer loyalty?

As a leader, if you fail to execute a strategy to answer the aforementioned points, your product is going to fail to meet its true potential. You will end up having a product with a reduced shelf life, excess inventory, and with an untimely entry to the decline stage. It is essential to understand that every product is unique, and they spend different amounts of time in each stage of the product lifecycle. Each stage has its own costs, risks, and opportunities, and the leader has to adapt and execute strategies accordingly.

For example, if your product is still at the launching stage, you have to plan for concept testing with real potential users. Now, at the initial stage, you will encounter the problem of costs without producing much income. So, the sword is hanging on your head regarding the budget. On the same note, market development can demand you anything from a brief sketch to a prototype of your product. You should have enough to show something to your potential investors and customers.

The next hurdle comes when you have to execute the plans for building product awareness and reaching your target market. You have to strategize based on the complexity of your product, competition, how new and innovative the product is, etc. Your sales team should be equipped enough to perform product optimization in the market.

As your product slowly grabs the market, your plans should shift from getting attention from consumers to establishing a brand presence. To be ahead of the competition, you have to plan to add new features to your product, strengthen your support services, and open new distribution channels. On the contrary, when your product reaches the maturity stage, your strategies must shift toward reducing the price to stay competitive.

However, it is again challenging to maintain a balance with profit margin. You have to effectively strategize to reduce the production cost while keeping the sales steady. It is challenging to make ongoing improvements to your product and let consumers know that the product is getting better. At the same time, you must be vigilant toward market saturation. Your plans must now focus on your strengths—differentiation, features, brand awareness, price, and customer service to become the brand of choice.

Now, with constantly changing market needs, your product is bound to enter the decline stage. It can be due to too much competition or outdated technology, or loss of customer interest. For example, Heinz introduced EZ Squirt colorful ketchup in 2000. Initially, it was a huge success, but the novelty wore off, and the product failed. The market is volatile, and consumers are fickle with their tastes.

As a leader, you can seek newer ways to grow and come out of that decline phase. For example, Pepsi extended its product line by adding cherry, vanilla, and other flavors. Listerine was repackaged and rebranded to become a mouthwash that cures bad breath. Also, there is another way to go back to the beginning of the product lifecycle and bring in a whole new dimension, much like Nintendo, which went from making video arcade games to video game systems for personal use.

The prime focus during this journey of ideation to execution is to understand the characteristics of each stage and employ various market research tools to analyze growth rate, sales trends, competition, and pricing to pinpoint the type of strategies you need to execute. According to business experts, there are some key strategies that no leader can escape from execution.

- Establishing competitive edge: A plan to establish your brand as the expert.
- Building pricing strategy: Brace your company with changing pricing strategy.
- Creating a unique market strategy: Explore different channels to connect to the target audience.

Another critical aspect includes the factors that affect your product's survival in the market, and a leader must ponder upon the following:

- Are you entering a highly competitive market?
- Is your team technically competent enough to execute every strategy while the technology evolves?
- Have you done enough market research to analyze the rate of market acceptance for your product?
- Are you braced against economic turmoil? Change in trade policy or pandemic, maybe.

Leadership skills don't differ based on the timeline you spend as a leader. Whether you are a leader for 15 minutes or 15 years, you will be thrown into a miasma of challenges where you cannot escape from dealing with ongoing project constraints, such as time, budget, quality, and scope. Additionally, challenges crop up due to constant pressure from team members and stakeholders and, of course, from the changing market scenario. Lack of detailed planning, consistent processes and methodologies, improper management of stakeholders, and budget overruns are some of the key problems that hinder execution strategies. If you take a closer look, any execution fails due to three main causes – People, Process, and Communication. As a leader, constructing strategy is vital for the growth of the organization; however, executing those strategies amongst the three main barriers to growth is the hardest part. An incredible leader focuses on how to execute incredibly.

No matter how bright an idea you conceive, it shall lose its sheen until you execute it; because *Vision without execution is a daydream. Execution without vision is a nightmare.*

Facts about Overcoming the Hurdles

Problem: Misinterpretation of ideas/strategies
Solution: Every individual is unique in their perceptive skills. There is a number of ways your team can interpret your idea and your execution plans. The key lies in effective communication, well-planned visualization of future prospects, and you being a patient listener to others' views.

Problem: Misalignment of goals and business objectives
Solution: Develop a business case, which essentially studies and communicates the business value and financial benefits of executing a particular strategy.

Problem: Lack of accountability
Solution: Accountability is one of the first rules of execution. Every member of the team has an integral role to play in producing the outcome successfully. Even a single person lacking accountability can cause a ripple effect. Define roles and responsibilities for everyone.

Problem: Optimism Bias
Solution: You and your team may be talented but do not fall prey to optimism bias. Not all that glitters is gold. Do all the risk assessments. Closely monitor and control the schedule and timeline and ensure its visibility to team members, stakeholders, and executives to keep everyone on the same page.

Not every great idea can make you a millionaire. Be realistic toward the market needs.

Problem: Struggle with budgeting.
Solution: Create a detailed list of all the required resources and the skills needed to accomplish them, and evaluate the existing resource/skill gap before jumping into execution.

Problem: Scope-Creep!!! When stakeholders do not know their needs.
Solution: When you struggle to meet a stakeholder's new demands or instructions that weren't part of the planning phase, then you have to collect more information, gather requirements, draft specifications, and, above all, clearly identify the goals. Prepare your team for the change management process but also communicate to the client about how last-minute changes impact the project/product.

Problem: Insufficient risk management
Solution: Not to scare the leaders, but they should identify all potential risks before executing any plan. Categorize them and create measures on how to respond if/when a risk crops up.

Remember, without execution, and you are just weaving a beautiful delusion.

The Little Idea of Selling Your Vision

Have you ever watched Shark Tank? The bottom line is to make something that gets everyone's attention. Executing an idea into a fruitful outcome requires you to help others understand your vision. Is it so easy to sell your vision? Huh! Then, everyone would have become Steve Jobs or Bill Gates. Selling vision is like trying to disrupt normalcy, trying to introduce a change that people may or may not like. It is all about making money; no business works on charity.

Your value proposition should be defined clearly enough that your team and other stakeholders realize that the idea shall generate revenue. Selling lofty ideas without showcasing their ability to reap financial results will never get you the right audience. Simplicity is the key when you sell your idea. Remember, people are not waiting to hear your language jargon; rather, they are running short of time. They want to know the benefits.

Your team members wish to know how the execution of your vision can bring overall benefits to the organization while your customers would concentrate more on their needs getting fulfilled. On the other hand, investors would like to have their money invested in something productive. Making it easy for someone on the outside to understand what you are trying to accomplish invariably creates engagement and increases your chances of expanding buy-in for your idea.

Piece together your idea appropriately, strategize on the route of effective communication and refine your message so much so that they all know what you are doing and what they have to do, and how all are in the same win-win situation.

Key Takeaways:

- Ideation to execution needs effective planning and strategies
- Not all ideas can be transformed into a great product
- Setting executable milestone is essential
- Understand your team's potential, resource availability and market demands
- Execution fails due to People, Process, and Communication
- Get rid of optimism bias

9

C FOR CAPACITY, NOT COMPETITION

"No one can whistle a symphony. It takes a whole orchestra to play it."
— H.E. Luccock

Curiosity has always been the instrument behind humans' growth. A few curious minds came together, brewed innovative ideas, and worked out strategies; while a few ideas failed, a couple turned into a miracle, and there, a successful business house was built. Take a closer look, and you will discover the various C's involved in an organization's growth. Culture, Curiosity to discover newer avenues, Capacity to grow, and above all, building a Competitive Edge to sustain in the competitive market. Growth remains the ultimate motive for any organization. As the market grows and competitors crop up from every nook and corner, the very first idea that takes an organization by storm is to go ahead with the competition. Fiercely reciprocating toward competition by delving into a prospering zone has become the first choice for every leader to retain their niche in the growing market.

Reality Check!!! There stands a concrete misjudgment about equating competition with success.

Samsung and iPhone are two major players in the cell phone domain. Do they compete with each other? Never. Both giants are busy refining their own capacity to retain their loyal customer base. Growth should be knitted as an inherent ideology. The market competition indeed reveals the stark realities of the business world and imparts better scopes to ideate new products and strategies; however, better growth is possible only by improving your inherent and ingrained capacity.

Enhancing the production capacity by adding new and better features, honing the teams' proficiency through upskilling, and building better brand value for the organization are some of the better options to sustain in a competitive market. No man is an island, and no organization can thrive without concentrating on improvising its team, strategies, and product. It is essential to remember that competition is eternal; no amount of competitive edge can seal your fate with permanent success. The only thing that ensures continued progress is your inherent capacity and your willingness to enhance that capacity in every segment of your organizational culture.

Have you ever seen an anthill? It is the mounded nest of ants that they build out of dirt or sand. It seems to be a mere nest, but if you dig a little deeper, you will discover a serpentine route under the ground, nothing less than a maze. The anthill that appears only a few inches to the eyes actually goes deep enough, more than two times its superficial appearance.

Precisely, an anthill is more of a doorway to a whole series of organized tunnels and nests. Surprisingly, within an anthill, you may end up finding several small anthills independently working out their roles. Additionally, there is also an interesting concept of shaping the anthill into a specific, deliberate shape, most of the time to escape predators. Ants act and build. An anthill bears a fascinating analogy with an organizational structure.

Labor is divided, roles are defined, goals are set, and strategies are well-planned in advance to reach the set milestone. If we delve into a closer observation of the working principle of ants, we can easily decipher the significance of the capacity building. Ants do not waste time in comparing their colonies with termites or other species of ants or insects. They know their job well and keep refining their course of action. If you observe a chain of ants moving with their sugar cubes, they are not deterred by any hindrance. Even if you put another sugar cube at another angle, you won't find an ant coming out of that chain and chasing the other sugar cube.

Oh! That's weird, you would say. An extra sugar cube is an added benefit; it is foolish to ignore that. However, ants do not function like that. It is not like they don't need that extra sugar cube. It is just about finishing the task at hand first and then looking at the other alternative and eventually deciding on the profitability score. A business organization more or less works on the same principle of efficiently reaching the prime objective first. The less you get distracted, the sooner you can reach the set milestone.

Let's say you have started your entrepreneurship journey with a fintech business that basically bridges the gap of small-scale women-run businesses with various funding sources. Over a period of time, your app gets a lot of attention, and you could do well for your business as well as for women entrepreneurs. Eventually, a KPO initiative draws much attention in the market as its prime objective is to educate women about entrepreneurship. So, basically, they indulge in the complete definition of entrepreneurship rather than focusing only on the funding part.

Now, on considerable lending thought, you find this KPO a huge competition because, according to you, if an entrepreneur is taught everything about the whole process of approaching incubators, angel investors, and venture capitalists, they will never use your technology. So, what do you do? You invest your time, resources, and your energy to develop a competitive app in the edtech sector to fight this KPO. Fair enough.

But then, your inherent customers who were educated enough about the process of entrepreneurship discover your lack of interest in helping them get in touch with the funding sources through your fintech business. You and your team now indulge more in educating people about entrepreneurship rather than focusing on the existing businesswomen. Eventually, while trying to build your niche in a new domain, you forget to enhance your existence in your actual game. The fintech product loses its sheen as your app is no longer updated, your customer interface is no longer available to address your customers' concerns, and you no longer advertise your interest in that fintech segment.

On the one hand, you lose your brand value and customer base for that fintech company, and on the other hand, you face tremendous budgetary constraints and face problems bridging the skill gap and resource allocation for the new initiative. In short, you start again from scratch without reaping any benefit from your previous endeavor. Being the leader, you can now fathom the mishap the organization is facing; however, you cannot step back, considering so many people's jobs are at stake. You hatch a new idea of recruiting some specifically skilled people from the market who have prior experience with edtech apps.

Initially, your existing team is excited to have new people on board and starts looking forward to ending the task well in advance. However, the newly recruited ones develop a cultural conflict with the existing team while many old members find themselves not getting enough jobs in hand. The whole company slowly gets divided into groups as the difference in work ethics, style and performance become apparent. The old staff feel demotivated and start leaving the company; with conflict rising every now and then, productivity is reduced, and eventually, the company shuts down. In the end, neither the booming business of fintech could fetch the fate it deserved, nor the new endeavor with an ed-tech app could end up anywhere. Amid all the pandemonium of conflict and competition, your entrepreneurial endeavor got ruined.

If we take a closer look, every company in the market has its own wallet share. Whether you are running a hundred employees' organization or you are as big as Microsoft, you definitely have a specific market share where you thrive with the help of loyal customers, vendors, suppliers, and other stakeholders. Additionally, your product's specific features add value to your market share. As stated above, iPhone has its own customer base, and so is Samsung. Their vendors may be the same or different, but they do work out different strategies for different companies. In retrospect, if/when you are given a particular market share, it is essential to keep holding onto it and enhancing it further instead of dwelling on something new every now and then just because the neighbor is doing it.

Concentrating on competition is very similar to every parent wanting their children to become an engineer. Society needs good doctors to save lives, administrators to run the system, intellectuals to make policies, and of course, engineers to build technology. Much like how a neurosurgeon cannot fetch great results in the IT industry, you, as a leader, cannot entertain every kind of business proposal to grow your organization. If an organization's success depends on the proficiency of the team, it is imperative to concentrate more on building the capacity of the team and optimum resource planning. Once your capacity as an organization is enhanced, you will automatically have your competitive edge.

Capacity planning, enhancement, and optimum utilization can never be ignored by leaders. Let's consider the capacity enhancement of human resources. As a leader, you must know the demand for resources and who is on the payroll in order to effectively plan and execute a task, and who is the most suitable candidate to accomplish it. Building on your team's capacity can help you accurately calculate the velocity of your team, discover the hurdles, find out where strengths gleam and whether burnout is looming. Even in this aspect of leadership, measurement is the key to managing and enhancing team capacity. When an organization focuses on capacity building over competing in the market, it chalks out a better path to growth through a multitude of ways.

One of the essential benefits of capacity planning and organization is the maximum utilization of resources. Every company struggles with resource availability and allocation challenge. The resource is not only about budget availability but also about the existing skills within the team or features within your product. A leader must have a clear view of what is available to accomplish the task. By maximizing your utilization, you can get more done with the same amount of people, which increases your chances for success and on-time delivery.

Let's assume you run a company of content writing which specifically focus on business writing skills. Your team is doing well, but one fine day you decide to try your hand at academic writing. Instead of looking for talent outside the organization, you get to know about two existing content writers who have been proficient in academic writing in their previous job. You can effectively start the academic writing unit on a small scale using your two existing talents. It is a classic case of maximum utilization of resources. As a leader, if you know the strengths and weaknesses of your team, you can chalk out various ways to bridge the gap. Also, as you start this diversification on a small scale, you don't lose your main business focus.

But then, starting and continuing a new business proposal with a handful of few may invite new troubles. What if your lead performer falls sick? Should your whole team suffer by failing to meet the target? No. Once you focus on capacity building, you will always have real-time data available on your whole team and availability/dearth of the required skill set. When you know your team in and out, you can plan well before nudging on a different domain. Entering into competition often looks more lucrative than honing your inherent capacity because if you go ahead with the competition and emerge as a bigger success, it designs a better prospect for the organization. And to combat this competition, diversification becomes a good weapon. But here, one critical argument is, do all diversification work wonders?

During the 1970s, National Semiconductor Corporation tried to make electronic consumer products along with semiconductors that went inside them. Interestingly, they overlooked their suitability and capacity for retail manufacturing. Eventually, it was crushed by companies that were more suitable for retail manufacturing. By the time digital watches became popular in America, NSC was ousted from the marketplace while suffering huge losses that again outshone its success in the field of semiconductors. Entering a competition should be well-planned. Firstly, a strategic move should focus on the core abilities and strengths of the company while keeping the budget in mind. One should not enter a competition just for the sake of it. There should be a strategy behind it. It should be controlled diversification and, of course, informed. Strong brands often exploit competitors' weaknesses by enhancing their own capacity. In the business world, it is often said that even during tough times, it is always better to stick to what you know best.

Have you ever seen a Panipuri guy switching to a sandwich business just because the market has churned out demand over continental and European cuisines? Never. He would rather go in and incorporate different flavors into his Panipuri platter. Additionally, if he wishes to grow his business by putting extra stalls or making a chain, he would concentrate on building a team who are the best in his business. Diversification is indeed needed, but you should be clear about your strong domains first. Also, is it worth switching all your resources to uncharted domains just because the other person is reaping benefits from it? As you remain watchful toward your own capacity, you tend to plan better with accurate forecasting for your resources and projects, which means a greater probability of hitting deadlines.

Focusing on competition invariably leads to untimely burnout because you get very little time to prove your mettle. Your team is eventually pushed too far beyond its capacity, which in turn leads to physical and emotional burnout. As you focus on capacity, you get the power to flag potential overages before they become a larger problem.

Many teams employ a project backlog for tasks once they hit their threshold. Similarly, as your business grows in your original domain, you realize as and when additional people are needed in the team. Also, the more you talk about building capacity, team members become productive as they know exactly what they should be working on. Focusing on capacity help, you plan out time and tasks so that the workload is well distributed. Working in your capacity as a team leads to a well-oiled team that can best serve the clients, keep your product viable and sustainable in the market, and your team remains abreast with the changing market.

"Of the top 10 sources of innovation, employees are the only resource that you can control and access that your competitors cannot. Employees are the one asset you have that can actually be a sustainable competitive advantage."
— Kaihan Krippendorff

Essentially, it is not about getting allured by your competitor; but building your survival strategy. Sustenance of business occurs by building a competitive advantage which is again an outcome of honing your capacity. There are multiple ways for a company to produce goods or deliver services better than its competitors. The idea for any business is to achieve superior margins and generate value for the company and its different stakeholders. Therefore, when an organization builds on its capacity, it creates a uniqueness that cannot be replicated by competitors in the market. Capacity enhancement improves the organization internally and sets the business apart from its competition. The most wonderful benefit of capacity building is the creation of brand value in the eyes of the consumers.

Let me share my experience here. With our edtech initiative, we have launched products that impart comprehensive solutions to every educational need under one roof. In the last couple of years, our team could build a prominent niche in the market, and our customers are happy with the kind of service we provide.

Now, as we are continuously improvising our product and services based on customers' feedback, they are content with the kind of service they are getting. Having said that, are we immune to the competition? Never. With technology evolving every day, and innovation rearing its head from every corner, we are surrounded by competitors who are trying to do something unique.

However, if we look through customers' perspectives, change is not welcomed that easily. If you as a customer have got used to android phones, you will be reluctant to switch to any other kind of phone, even if iPhone20 comes to the market.

Our customers have got used to our products and their features and do share a comfortable relationship with the customer service interface. Welcoming a new company (with or without a similar product) is more like starting everything all over again. And believe me, people are lazy to do so once they have reached their comfort zone. Our customers are happy with our capacity to entertain and solve their concerns. So, the more we work on enhancing our own skills, the more we widen our safer zone of operation.

Creating a competitive advantage or enhancing your capacity is like building a protective fosse. It helps in creating sustained success for a business and attracting capital more readily and cheaply. There are many ways to improve your capacity without imitating what your competitors are doing in the market. You can invest in upskilling your workforce, be it the technical team or the customer interface team. You can shift to a better vendor to achieve your resource goals. You can invest in technological renovation for your product. And the list grows and proliferates in every aspect of product development and customer retention and satisfaction. At the end of the day, it is the company's value proposition that makes it stand out. As a leader, you have to clearly identify the features or services that make your company or product attractive to customers. It must offer real value in order to generate interest.

Do you know why Tata products are so valued amongst customers? There lies a fragrance of patriotism, humanity, and authenticity in whatever they launch in the market. On the same note, Reliance Industries nudge on the emotions of middle-class mentality. They vouch for affordability. Every company must establish its target market to further ensure best practices that will help in its future growth. Similarly, you must know and define your competitors in the marketplace.

Let's say you are focused on the food industry. In one of those glittering events of awarding the businessman of the year, someone from the fintech gets an award. You, too, wish to become businessman of the year someday, but does that mean you have to jump into the fintech industry to win that prestigious award? No. Essentially, you as a leader have to identify your company's value proposition that will be sought after by the target market because it cannot be replicated by competitors.

Many giants of the business world have survived over the decades by employing different strategies of capacity building and retention. For example, Walmart has won the market with a cost leadership strategy. Their motto is *Always Low Prices* through economies of scale and the best available prices of a good. Their goal has always been to become the lowest-cost manufacturer or provider of a good or service. They kept on producing goods that were of standard quality for consumers at a price that was lower and more competitive than other comparable products. Does that mean Walmart's competitors are foolish? No. It simply secludes different customers for different brands. If you wish to build your capacity by incorporating a cost leadership strategy, then you will have to combine low-profit margins per unit with large sales volumes to maximize profit. You have to seek the best alternatives in manufacturing a good or offering a service and advertise this value proposition which your competitors cannot replicate.

On the other hand, Apple uses a differentiation strategy to allure its consumer base. With iconic designs, and innovative technologies, Apple's products are highly sought-after products, and consumers are willing to pay a premium for Apple devices. You can indeed build your capacity on differentiation strategy, too, by developing unique goods or services that are significantly different from competitors. Making such an attempt would need you to invest more in your R&D team to maintain or improve the key product or service features. By offering a unique product with a totally unique value proposition, businesses can often convince consumers to pay a higher price which results in higher margins.

Nevertheless, focusing on the key aspect is essential before you plan for capacity building. If you think you have a niche market, then are you focused enough to decipher the changing needs of your niche market? One of the core foci of any business is customer retention. What if your loyal customers are allured by a similar product that is your cheaper alternative? Now, your customer is concerned about the cost of your product, and thus you, too, have to focus on your cost amendment strategy. Is it possible to sell the same quality at a reduced price? Becoming the lowest-cost producer in a concentrated market segment is a good strategy to remain sustainable within your target audience.

However, a reduction in price is not always possible, and there you must focus on your differentiation strategy. You build customized or specific value-add products in a narrow-targeted market segment. For example, Whole Foods Market's advantage relies on a differentiation focus strategy. The company is a leader in the premium grocery market and charges more premium prices because its products are unique. This is appealing to a niche market with higher disposable income. You can build your capacity on this strategy once your company achieves customer loyalty. This strategy will not work if your competitors can copy the unique features of the product. In some cases, the characteristics of the competitors' products might be similar, but if you employ effective positioning, your product will be perceived as something unique.

Building on capacity is not equivalent to growing your workforce from hundreds to thousands or increasing your operations by two folds. Honing your capacity is all about becoming a differentiator. While you tread into your domain, you must be aware of your key differentiator. What is your expertise in the field you have chosen?

The narrower your expertise is, the easier it will be to establish your credibility with your potential customers. Keep evaluating your strengths, weaknesses, reputation, and the area where your company reaps better benefits. You have to keep refining your brand's story and the company's history to determine the features that make you unique.

Along with this, your focus must shift to your product as well. What makes your product different? The production process, packaging, or materials? Moreover, if your product design and process involved are too simple, you will soon invite a lot of competition. Thus, you cannot refrain from refining your product. While building on your capacity, you have to ensure that your offerings meet the needs of the target audience. Similarly, you will have to keep looking for the best way to communicate your expertise to clients. Use surveys and interviews to collect information about the features of the product people are looking for. Once you have determined the differentiators, you can easily scrutinize the potential customers' responses to correct the strategy.

> *"You have to do things right to stay in business, and that's not easy, and that's a choice on a daily basis, the choices you make in how to run your business and how to have a point of differentiation and how to be true to your brand, how to offer something that people want and to offer something that you love."*
> —Venus Williams

Every now and then, as the market scenario changes, you have to redefine your value proposition based on different differentiators like price, reputation, brand image, product, service, relationship, or distribution. This will, in turn, help you position your statement by focusing on the essential characteristics. Your message should underline the value you provide to customers, the problems your product solves, the advantages it delivers, and the reason to choose your brand over the other players in the market.

On the same note, storytelling is another crucial step to sustain in the market. Does your company have a story that sets you apart from the other players in the market? It can be about your mission, values, ethics, or the kind of workforce you have.

Storytelling is the most powerful tool to build customer loyalty and encourage consumers to build a relationship with your brand. The success of Toms Shoes reflects upon capacity building through the power of storytelling. They entered an extremely competitive industry with products similar in many respects, including quality, price, and style. The brand told the story of the founder Blake Mycoskie who was traveling in Argentina in 2006 and witnessed the hardships faced by children growing up without shoes. Since that time, the $625 million company has managed to donate 50 million shoes to children in need, provided more than 250,000 weeks of safe water in six countries, and restored sight to over 360,000 people.

The last and crucial step to capacity building is taking effective actions. If you are a proud owner of a differentiator factor, show it off to the world by producing results. Building your capacity is not a one-time job, done and dusted. It is a continuous process. Keep monitoring your products' performance and customers' responses after improvising on your capacity. We are thriving in a hyper-competitive market, and to sustain ourselves, every business must strive to gain an advantage over the competition. Buyers are savvy, so much so that research has proven that 86% of buyers are likely to check out your competitors at any given point in time. There is only one route to survive – avoid competition and build on competitive advantage.

The moment you shift your prime focus to capacity building, the pointer goes straight to what your customers feel about your company as a whole. As you concentrate on building a high-performing team, it not only helps in productivity and cost reduction but also ensures customer retention. Similarly, when you are looking for a competitive advantage, it seems easy to go for known niches where customers are easily found. However, an under-serviced niche can fetch you a market advantage.

In my case, we did not change the education system per se. We didn't propose a different definition of photosynthesis or proposed a different curriculum altogether. Rather we focused on the problem of bringing everything under one single roof, which was not available to the schools. In our pursuit, competition became few, and we could establish brand recognition early.

While considering capacity building in the scope of the customer, it is important to understand the DNA footprint of your ideal customer. Not every customer is the same. If ten people are buying from you, that doesn't mean your product or customer base does not need any enhancement. Target the right customer, remain vigilant of their buying process, and be informed with their decision-making; this will help your sales team, and post-sales support teams win business and retain lifelong customers. When customers feel that you understand them and you, too, serve them exactly what they need at the very time that they need it, they will place you above any competition. Always use your strengths in a more innovative and creative way to gain more customers and tap into new markets.

Even under stiff competition, when you focus on capacity building, you develop a competitive advantage that provides you with greater opportunities to close more business. More importantly, the stronger your inherent capacity and competitive advantage, the greater your ability to sustain a position of strength in the market, no matter its conditions or level of competition.

Beyond the concept of team and customer, the most integral part of the capacity building happens in the scope of product improvement. Bringing about significant changes in your product features to get new clients, retain existing users, and even recapture lost customers is considered product improvement. Many business houses add fresh features, or they choose to upgrade the existing ones. Continuous updates make the current product more advanced and, in turn, enhance the value proposition and expand the customer base. Additionally, it provides more value to existing customers, reduces churn rate, and contributes to building brand loyalty.

Now, there can be intentional improvement once you find out why customers will continue to use your product. For example, Oppo and Vivo encash the basic human emotions of photography and keep on introducing their new products with better camera resolution.

But then, there have to be regular tweaks like WhatsApp and other mobile apps regularly asking the customers to update the software for better functioning. Introductory improvement is often made to make it easier for new customers.

Either way, innovation or changing product features is a risky affair. You will never know which step backfires. As Steve Jobs once said — *You can't just ask customers what they want and then try to give that to them. By the time you get it built, they'll want something new.*

Cracking the Myths around Capacity Building

Are you sure of your customers' needs?

Always embrace an effective customer communication channel to know what they truly want. For example, your customers can pat you for your proposal to build a house for them on Mars. But are they aware of the pros and cons of the whole idea?

Have you identified your pain points?

Just because your customer wants a cell phone at meager 10 Rupees, you cannot jump to satisfy that demand. Sit and do your research well. How financially viable is it to make a product that your loyal customer wants? Is your existing team capable of making the changing demand? And more than anything, will your effort be aligned with your organization's ultimate motive?

Check on your competitors but don't get trapped.

Steve Jobs or Bill Gates, or many such millionaires, have enough money to switch to any field of business they wish to go. But is Bill Gates trying to transform Microsoft into McDonalds'? No. As a leader, you should keep your company's core focus intact and keep advancing in the same domain. Diversification is good but should not be drastic.

Focus on product differentiation

Even if you take a plunge into a competitive domain, you have to work harder toward product differentiation. Why do you think GPay is better than Paytm? GPay is KYC compliant and provides cashback and rewards. It is direct from a bank account and has multilingual support. In fact, the app speed is higher for GPay.

Is your vision connected to practice?

When you articulate a clear vision of your product, it becomes easier to earn customers' approval. As you share your enthusiasm, it makes it more possible for others to play a crucial role in the whole product improvement process. Always communicate your thoughts with marketing and sales teams or developers to express your intention about changes. Remember, the upgrading process will always need a strategic basis.

Have you specified your metrics?

For example, if you design an app, consider the DAU metric and if you run a SaaS product, take MAS (monthly active subscribers) into account. While for a marketplace business, you have to find a correlation between supply and demand.

How dedicated is your team?

Capacity building cannot happen without a dedicated team. You must have a data-driven, user-centric, and willing to innovate team.

Are you building your capacity on the right note?
Capacity building needs financial, operational, and also an emotional investment. The most critical question is, why are you enhancing your capacity? Is it to move ahead with the change or just to satiate a handful of customers or competitors? Focus on your right users, the team that has worked hard to bring you success to date, and the strategies that seem to be out of place, and then decide on the scope of capacity building.

When Competition Killed

Swiggy and Zomato had their fair share of failures, and still, they could withstand the competition amongst themselves and even came out as a warrior during the pandemic. At present, they remain the giants amongst the food tech startup. However, in 2015, Dazo, a Bangalore-based startup, emerged as a "food on demand" company, and it partnered with a few selected restaurants. It took care of the food delivery logistics. Their policy was to let hungry customers find and order their perfect meal within seconds of opening the app. Dazo strategized its operation by analyzing and saving users' behavior, preferences, and direct feedback. Much like how Zomato works. A counter-intuitive approach was about working with only about 20 restaurants that offered different cuisines. They believed that hungry customers had no patience for going through dozens of restaurants' menus and reviews and preferred delivering the best food within minutes for an affordable price.

However, the competition was fierce in this sector, while lack of funding too remained a concern for Dazo's smooth functioning. Heavy capital investment is essential in the food-tech industry. Additionally, Dazo had entered into a zone of high competition, and to sustain, they chose to slash their prices so much so that practically no company could make substantial revenue. Eventually, with Swiggy and Zomato thriving, client acquisition became a problem. And within a year of launch, Dazo vanished from the market.

Key Takeaways:
- Focus on capacity building first
- Focusing exclusively on competition leads to untimely burnout
- Capacity building helps in building competitive edge

CONCLUSION

Let me put it straight without borrowing any magnanimous quote on great leadership—no organization can ever lick the sweet nectar of success without effective leaders. Any organization's growth, development, profitability, and sustainability materialize under the umbrella of effective leadership only. Believe it or not, every second you spend leaning on your glorious success stories of the past, there is someone somewhere eagerly hatching an innovative idea. Innovative disruption is the stark reality of today's business world. Before even you can celebrate the success of your high-performing team and your awesome product, the market will offer you a new set of competition; in the form of an evolved product, changing customer demands, and continuously advancing technology.

Ignorant are those who say leaders are born. In today's world, leaders are made from scratch. Effective leaders are chiseled with time to shine like a diamond with continuous learning and embracing change and strategic execution of plans.

We humans often fail to make any sense of small efforts. We fail to see the importance of laying one brick at a time to build a concrete wall. When a pebble is cast into a pond, ripples spread in all directions; it doesn't depend on the type of pebble but the style of throwing it. Leadership skill is like that pebble; you may hold a prestigious degree and all the desired (bookish) traits of a great leader; however, your effectiveness is determined by your style of dispersing those leadership traits.

Leadership skills are neither inherited nor gifted but bestowed upon you through a continuum of the process of learning, unlearning, and relearning. Trials and tribulations are part and parcel of a leader's life, which no one can escape. Irrespective of your prestigious educational qualification and a long list of past accolades, the fickle world is going to measure you for your present results.

Are you able to translate the organization's goal into reality? Does your team accept you as their mentor? Do you know your people, process, and product well enough to represent the whole organization? Are you open to change while clinging to the organization's vision? There remains an unending list of questions for you to answer before you desire to become an effective leader. Leadership does not proliferate at the top of the hierarchy but in the efficiency of the leader to build a high-performing team and move along with it.

Prestige, power, and popularity are often misquoted as the essence of leadership. Indeed, holding the reign is a matter of prestige, and it bestows a sizeable amount of power and popularity. However, the true value of leadership is much beyond that. Leadership is about spreading your thoughts, words, and actions to every nook and corner of the organization to extract the right talent to reach the desired goal. Sitting down, leaning, and relaxing in that cozy chair of an air-conditioned office and dictating to people to perform a task are definitions of an era bygone. The present world is witnessing change faster than anticipated and is embracing innovation not only for product design but also in the way teams are built and performed, and leadership is exhibited.

Becoming a leader always seems to be a lucrative option, and invariably we all wish to sit on that pinnacle someday. Honestly, it feels good to be like that snake sitting on top of the anthill and oozing out power and strength.

But as soon as the reality of growth and development stings, one gets to know how sitting and ruling can never be an accepted norm. Leadership is a multi-hued, distinctly layered, strategically built, and there is too much work to do.

Holding vision in mind, tirelessly striving to transform that vision into reality, empowering everyone around by unlocking their true potential, nourishing an indomitable organizational culture, handling conflict with care, and never hesitating to embrace the changing market scenario. Leadership is not just about being at the top but a conflicting and challenging task that needs a steady supply of patience, passion, and perseverance. True leaders do not wake up on one fine day and declare themselves impatient and devoid of passion. If at all they do so, they sow the seed of an irrevocable peril for the whole organization.

Every organization is built on the premise of a vision that defines the envisaged future interposed by ambition and the prevailing resources and opportunity. And the leader remains the visionary who can clearly define and pursue the vision even in the wake of prevailing dearth and leverage available resources and opportunities at all times. However, it is not enough for the leader to be visionary but clueless on how to utilize the existing endowment of resources to realize the vision. It is not enough for a leader to be visionary and still fail to lead by example to inspire the rest of the followers to the achievement of the vision. It is never enough for a leader to sit at the top and yet fail to communicate to the rest of the team members to amalgamate efforts to the realization of the vision.

In this constantly evolving world of business, leaders need to drape many avatars apart from being just visionary. Building an upskilled, highly competent team who understands the true value of organizational goals is not a one-day delegation. In the present times, when continued innovation is forming the core of every organization, leaders must build a dynamic team with a myriad of skills. With the rise in competition and customer expectations, building a high-performing team that can enhance the product and also widens and retains the customer base is a crucial and laborious task for every leader. Enhancing the team's performance and renovating the product based on the growing market need an uninterrupted flow of knowledge for the leaders themselves. They must learn and become the change champions.

Being cocooned at the top of the hierarchy might help you witness the changing world; however, without participating in this process of change, you cannot set the vision and team on track. Every leader must embrace a strategic change management process from inception to institutionalizing change to ensure that the change efforts pay off. But then, change is welcomed and embraced by credible leaders who display their authenticity and authority through their well-informed attitude and performance.

Come what may, leadership demands continued learning, and if there is ever a full stop in learning, leaders are shackled by an incessant pause in their growth curve. The more the leaders learn, the more up-to-date they become with the market's changing demands, product performance, and customer base. The more they are informed, the more prolific their performance becomes.

It is a common misconception that leadership is all about authority. Indeed, leaders are authorized to take the strategic call and decide the organization's fate; however, authority is a decorated term for the assigned role. Even managers have a certain amount of authority in their hands, and management is an integral part of the success of an organization. However, there is a prominent line of difference between management and leadership. The latter is a process of social influence that has the potential to maximize others' efforts toward the achievement of a greater good. How could a leader do that? Because a learned leader knows the dire necessity of proving his credibility before disposing of his authority.

Organizations are built with human resources, and any performing human mind would like to take orders from a credible source. With continuous learning, leaders strengthen their credibility. But then, doubt always looms around the corner. Do credible leaders get the luxury of learning early in their careers? No. Leaning in leadership is the biggest illusion one can ever have. The more you climb the ladder, the busier you must become; to learn more, grow beyond expectations, to plan beyond the prescribed limits. Leadership is polychromatic, where one shade highlights the power to direct and delegate, and the other shade reflects upon doing.

One of the key essentials of effective leadership lies in the leaders' ability to perform the action and pave the path for the team. An action-oriented leader not only guides the team in the right direction but also inspires others to become efficient performers. In essence, a leader's true value is never woven into his power of delegation but is integrated within his performance. A leader who performs empowers the rest of the team to perform with the same zeal and vigor. Empowering others needs a little bit of motivational intervention.

While it is necessary for a leader to be action-oriented, it doesn't mean that leaders should tailor-make solutions to every problem. Empowering the team means injecting problem-solving aptitude into everyone. Leaders must motivate others to act.

Now, we mortals have witnessed the rise and fall of innumerable leaders. Be it an enthralling speech by Martin Luther King Jr. or the gut-wrenching campaigning of Hitler, and great oration has always been the best asset of great leaders. As the world evolved, leadership styles, too, have undergone many transformations. Gone are the days of Iron-lady's authoritative style of leading.

Amidst the emergence of the gig economy and high-performers choosing to moonlight, laissez-faire and participative style of leadership has gained more prominence to retain skilled performers. Performers are no longer motivated by loud proclamations; rather, they want to see their leaders working hand in hand to solve real-life challenges. Leaders cannot script their role through their past achievements, while the present team is eager to scrutinize the present potential of the leaders. The present dynamic world of business wants leaders to be proactive on the field rather than being draped inside their glorious achievements of the past.

On the same note, present-day employees nourish a mindset of being self-made. They like to enjoy a little room for self-innovation and decision-making. They indeed want their leaders to show them the path but never want leaders to spoon-feed them. Because, with continued technological evolution and innovative disruption, obsoletion is happening faster than expected.

What worked in the past organization or in the past year may not be worth mentioning to the present team. An organization that intends to grow and proliferates in the market with beaming success needs its leaders to have more profound actions to showcase rather than mere anecdotes of their past achievements.

But then, if the dart points at action, leaders must be prepared for all kinds of repercussions. It is ridiculous but true that there are only three things that happen naturally in any organization. Confusion, Conflict, and Politics.

An improper and unplanned delegation of tasks creates confusion amongst the employees, which in turn kindles conflicting ideologies. And at the end, an otherwise healthy workplace starts reeking of organizational politics. One must understand that organizations are run by humans. The human mind is curious and creative at the same time. Although they are the harbinger of growth and development, a curious and creative mind is capable of chalking out many undesirable outcomes.

Where ideas grow, conflicting ideologies are watered too. However, leaders are always served with options. The growth of an organization is determined by leaders' attitude, whether they want to look for the problems or want to dig out the possibilities of growth amid the growing problems. As long as humans constitute the workforce, there can never be a politics-free organization. However, leaders can restrict the unwarranted proliferation of politics by shifting their focus to the various possibilities to grow with a high-performing team. Leadership is, after all, an embodiment that brings order and coordination in the performance of all employees to ensure the achievement of the set goals and vision.

On the same note, once the focus shifts toward possibilities, leaders fathom the strengths and weaknesses of every employee. Organizational politics can never be nipped; however, it indeed underlines the talent that can be extracted and exploited well for the betterment of the organization. Leadership is not about looking at the final result; it does need a human touch. Not every employee is verbose and believes in trumpeting their achievements.

There are many introverted high-performers who believe in making their work do the talk. Leaders must keep all their senses open to choose appropriate appreciation for the deserved ones. Biases are not meant for leaders; they are blinding. It is, of course, the leader's job to extract the full potential of the employees. But are you vigilant enough toward the authenticity of your team? Exhibiting talent and extracting talent are two distinct aspects, and leaders must do a reality check before opting for appreciation or criticism.

In this fast-paced world, leadership needs to be defined by results and not by mere attributes. Innovation and entrepreneurship are growing like weeds, and both leaders and employees believe in reaching their set targets. Hollowed motivational speeches do not make an iota of difference, but clear goals and strategic planning create wonders. Without clarity, even the brightest of employees cannot produce the desired outcome. The fact is ambiguity brews confusion and might lead to conflict. Clear goals, well-defined job descriptions, and properly chalked-out KPIs give the team a better picture of organizational goals. With clarity in delegation comes clarity in performance, and thus, the whole organization works in synchrony.

Presently, India is witnessing a sudden surge in entrepreneurship and a number of startups entering the unicorn club, and all of a sudden, building a business empire seems to be an easy job. However, is it so easy to transform any innovative idea into reality? 8 out of 10 startups fall flat within a year.

Hatching an idea is more like the mere conception of the life in a mother's womb. It can happen all of a sudden without any prior planning or intimation. However, transforming an idea into a profitable business is like giving birth to a child and then raising it appropriately. Whether it is an idea about a new product or a new marketing scheme, or a business strategy, raising it from being just an idea is a screwing factor. Without proper execution, every innovation falls flat. That top position of leadership comes with one of the loftiest responsibilities of strategic execution of every plan to reap benefits for the whole organization.

Now, hurdles shall always remain your constant companion while you execute any plan. Every plan you make will have its own set of resistance and also competition. How proficient are you in convincing the team and your customers toward your plan?

Not every proposal will be accepted at its face value. Leaders must be prepared for vehement rejection and also open to others' opinions. Similarly, when every organization in the market aspires to grow through innovation, competition is inevitable. Now, as a leader, should you entertain every kind of competition? Instead, leaders must focus on building a competitive edge by developing high-performing teams and product enhancement while retaining and widening the customer base. Leaders who focus on improvising their own skills and teams' capacity are able enough to build a competition-proof business strategy.

With so much power in hand and authority to dictate and delegate, leaders often develop a tendency to dominate and overpower others while forgetting the value of symbiotic relationships in building a successful organization. Sometimes, you, though being the leader, will no longer be the most intelligent person in the room. Sometimes, none of your past successful endeavors will come forward to help you solve the present problems. Sometimes, complex situations will not need complicated solutions but a simplifying quotient.

> "The true mark of a leader is the willingness to stick with a bold course of action — an unconventional business strategy, a unique product-development roadmap, a controversial marketing campaign — even as the rest of the world wonders why you're not marching in step with the status quo. In other words, real leaders are happy to zig while others zag. They understand that in an era of hyper-competition and non-stop disruption, the only way to stand out from the crowd is to stand for something special."
> — Bill Taylor

Effective leadership is about acting and building a team that knows what to do when to do and how to do it. When the business world is dynamic, the leaders, too, need to be dynamic and no longer remain cocooned in their comfort zone of delegating tasks. In essence, you cannot enjoy the luxury of being the snake who sleeps and rules. The business world is growing, and the leadership mindset is changing. Much like the ants, the present generation of businesses needs leaders who act and build.

Now, if you are bestowed with the crown of leadership; what would you like to become?

An Ant or a Snake?

Your success as a leader depends on what you choose today.

REFERENCES

1

- https://www.mbaknol.com/management-case-studies/case-study-how-netflix-took-down-blockbuster
- https://www.net360solutions.com/blog/kelloggs-won-cereal-war-great-depression

2

- https://www.siliconindia.com/shownews/5-worst-ceos-nid-98780-cid-100.html
- https://365pincode.com/apple-ceo-john-sculleys-worst-ever-decision/
- https://www.businessinsider.com/the-worst-ceos-in-american-history-2010-5?ir=t

3

- https://economictimes.indiatimes.com/news/company/corporate-trends/leadership-by-example-meritocracy-hardwork-discipline-honesty-are-the-only-ways-to-excel-globally-narayana-murthy-to-etilc

4

- https://www.forbes.com/sites/jackkelly/2021/12/16/the-story-behind-mcdonalds-former-ceo-returning-over-105-million-to-settle-a-dispute-over-allegations-of-multiple-consensual-sexual-activities/?sh=26f43bdb50ea
- https://www.investopedia.com/financial-edge/0113/5-most-publicized-ethics-violations-by-ceos.aspx
- https://www.failory.com/interview/adleaf-technologies

5

- https://businessjargons.com/organizational-conflict.html

6

- https://theleaderboy.com/sundar-pichai-personality-style-traits-qualities
- https://economictimes.indiatimes.com/news/company/corporate-trends/n-chandrasekaran-from-trainee-techie-to-two-time-tata-top-guy-heres-looking-back-at-a-glorious-career/articleshow/89503995.cms

7

- https://www.the-waves.org/2020/10/25/sustaining-innovation-failure-of-walkman/

8

- https://guttulus.com/15-reasons-why-compaq-failed/
- https://yourstory.com/smbstory/walmart-supplier-kitchenware-sanitiser-dispenser-coronavirus
- https://www.boredpanda.com/failed-products-innovationstechnology/?utm_source=google&utm_medium=organic&utm_campaign=organic

9

- https://www.referenceforbusiness.com/history2/40/national-semiconductor-corporation.html
- Porter, Michael E., "Competitive Advantage". 1985, Ch. 1, pp 11-15. The Free Press. New York.
- https://www.failory.com/cemetery/dazo

www.ingramcontent.com/pod-product-compliance
Lightning Source LLC
LaVergne TN
LVHW011418080426
835512LV00005B/137